The Authentic Church

D1127666

David Jackman is the Director of the Proclamation Trust, a London-based organisation involved in developing effective communication of the gospel. Previously, he was pastor of Above Bar Church in Southampton. For Christian Focus he has written two other titles: *Understanding the Church* and *Taking Jesus Seriously* (see end of this book for details). For other publishers he has written two commentaries – Judges and Ruth and the Letters of John– as well as a book on the Holy Spirit.

The Authentic Church

David Jackman

Christian Focus

BS
2725.3
-J33
1998

© David Jackman
ISBN 1 85792 197 6

Published in 1998
by
Christian Focus Publications,
Geanies House, Fearn, Ross-shire,
IV20 1TW, Great Britain.
Cover design by Donna Macleod

Scripture quotations, unless otherwise indicated, are from
The New International Version,
© 1973, 1978, 1984 by the International Bible Society.

Contents

Preface

I am grateful to the many colleagues and friends who have helped me in my attempts better to understand Paul's two letters to the Thessalonian church. In the summer terms of 1994 and 1995, the students of the Cornhill Training Course studied through the material with me, as we worked hard to discover the theme lines and their application to the contemporary church and world. Later that second summer, I had the privilege of visiting George Whitefield College and the Bible Training Institute of South Africa in Cape Town, where the material was re-worked with the students, and also a memorable ministers' seminar. Back in the UK, I was able to teach the letters to the congregation of St. Helen's, Bishopgate and on several weekends away for other churches. Finally, in the autumn of 1995 the present form of this material was developed for the annual autumn lectures of the Proclamation Trust, when for four mornings, ministers and Bible students from the London area and beyond met to study and discuss these two epistles.

Not only have I been greatly helped by penetrating questions, comments and suggestions from my hearers, at every stage of the process, but I have also benefited from other commentators, among which the volume by Charles A. Wanamaker in the New International Greek Testament Commentary series (1990) proved particularly helpful and stimulating.

Studying the Bible can often be a lonely business and we can feel very detached when we are doing that work. But actually, we are part of a great company of God's people all around the world now, and stretching back through the centuries of the church's history, who have worked at, and struggled with, the same inspired text as we do. Part of the fellowship we have in the gospel is the benefit of helping one another to do the job more effectively – to understand and apply God's unchanging Word to our lives and our moment in history. And this sort of co-operative study is based on the conviction that the best way to study (and preach or teach) the Bible is as it was originally given, by consecutive exposition, chapter by chapter, verse by verse. There is enormous value in getting a book of the Bible into our thinking, in the sense of really penetrating its inner life and purpose, so that we understand its structure and message. Then we can apply it, live it and teach it to others with conviction.

It is my hope and prayer that this book will provide that sort of stimulus and that the unique ingredients of the Thessalonian letters will become increasingly clear and urgent through its pages. May they increase in us the faith, love and hope that are to be the distinguishing characteristics of the people of God, as we move towards that great day when the Lord Jesus will return 'to be glorified in his holy people and to be marvelled at among all those who have believed' (2 Thess. 1:10).

David Jackman
London,
March, 1998

1

A Flagship Church

Thessalonica is still a populous and prosperous city, the second city in Greece after Athens, and the dominating presence in the north of the country. I have been privileged to meet with congregations of present-day Christian believers, the inheritors of the long tradition of gospel work and witness in the city, who love God's word and proclaim the good news of the Lord Jesus. There are some wonderful Christians today in the city, who have held firm to their faith in spite of continuing opposition, and who use all the opportunities of a modern cosmopolitan centre to reach others with Christ's love and truth. Tourism thrives in modern Thessalonica with its boulevard open-air cafes and its ancient sites and ruins. But just suppose that archaeologists could unearth a first century equivalent to today's promotional literature. Perhaps it would read something like this:

'Welcome to Thessalonica, capital of the Roman province of Macedonia, the largest and most prosperous city of northern Greece! Perhaps you have been fortunate enough to arrive in our city by ship. If so, you will have appreciated already our splendid natural harbour, and you will have noticed the multitude of trading ships from all over the empire. Perhaps you came by road – almost certainly by the Via Egnatia, the great imperial highway from Rome to the east, upon which our prosperous city occupies a key location. If you did come in by road, you won't have failed to notice the fertile plains that stretch all round the hinterland of our great city, with their crops, their fruit and vegetables, which stock the bustling markets in the city, and the latest Roman-style shopping mall, with its row of shops on the ground floor, coupled with living accommodation for the traders and their families above. So you can hardly have failed to be impressed by Thessalonica. It is a bustling, forward-looking, state-of-the-art, first century city. And you can hardly fail to be impressed by the huge range of temples and worship-shrines covering the whole pantheon of Graeco-Roman deities, and even including a synagogue for the invisible God of the Jews. Yes,

Thessalonica is the distinctive destination for the discerning, imperial traveller! Cosmopolitan, prosperous, above all it is a well-ordered city, loyal to Rome, a model of contemporary progress and security under the *Pax Romana*.'

Well, perhaps my calling isn't to write travel brochures! But it is into that sort of city Paul and Silas, probably accompanied by Timothy and perhaps by Luke as well, came unobtrusively, but with a remarkable message. They came as recent survivors of a severe flogging and a violent earthquake, about 90 miles away at Philippi, a Roman colony and garrison town. They came with a mission and a revolutionary message, and undeterred by what they had already suffered, they quickly set about their task.

To discover what happened we can turn to Acts 17:1-9, which not only provides an account of the history, but also some very important clues for us, as we begin to track down the purpose of Paul's correspondence with the infant church.

When they had passed through Amphipolis and Apollonia, they came to Thessalonica, where there was a Jewish synagogue. ²As his custom was, Paul went into the synagogue, and on three Sabbath days he reasoned with them from the Scriptures, ³explaining and proving that the Christ had to suffer and rise from the dead. 'This Jesus I am proclaiming to you is the Christ,' he said. ⁴Some of the Jews were persuaded and joined Paul and Silas, as did a large number of God-fearing Greeks and not a few prominent women.

⁵But the Jews were jealous; so they rounded up some bad characters from the market-place, formed a mob and started a riot in the city. They rushed to Jason's house in search of Paul and Silas in order to bring them out to the crowd. ⁶But when they did not find them, they dragged Jason and some other brothers before the city officials, shouting: 'These men who have caused trouble all over the world have now come here, ⁷and Jason has welcomed them into his house. They are all defying Caesar's decrees, saying that there is another king, one called Jesus.' ⁸When they heard this, the crowd and the city officials were thrown into turmoil. ⁹Then they put Jason and the others on bail and let them go.

This is a helpful and significant background passage for us, because getting back to Thessalonica is both easy and difficult. Easy – because we have a very straightforward account here recorded by Luke, of how the church began. But it is difficult, too, because within the two letters themselves the clues about the drive and purpose of the author in writing are buried in the text rather than being immediately obvious. So, we are going to have to do some digging in this first chapter, and the topsoil of Acts 17 is the best place to start.

As always, Paul's primary target in Thessalonica is the synagogue. Wherever there was an old covenant community, the apostle to the Gentiles invariably turned 'to the Jew first'. There is no record in history of an especially strong Jewish community in Thessalonica, though all the major cities in the first century Mediterranean world would have had groups of diasporan Jews, and it required only ten adult men for a synagogue to be formed. The remarkable note here in Luke's account, however, is the apparent brevity of Paul's ministry. He went into the synagogue (v. 2), and on three Sabbath days he reasoned with them from the Scriptures. The most natural meaning of this is that his stay was just under a month, which would seem to be an inordinately short time for the founding of a church as stable as this church in Thessalonica proved to be. In view of this, a number of scholars suggest that there may be a considerable time lapse, between verses 4 and 5 of Acts 17, during which Paul continued his mission, probably using Jason's house as his base, because that was where he was staying and clearly it was well known. Possibly this might have been in the mall of Roman shops which had recently been built, with their large living quarters attached. This type of house was called an *insula*, and was designed to provide both accommodation and a workplace. Certainly we read in verse 7 that Jason has welcomed them into his house, and we read in 1 Thessalonians itself, 2:9, that he worked night and day in order not to be a burden to anyone.

It may be that in those early days of the Gentile mission,

Paul was getting used to moving on quickly, and he just packed his time full instructing whoever was willing to listen as he worked on his tent-making. He had been requested to leave Philippi, and he was going to be hounded out of Thessalonica and not long after out of Berea (Acts 17:13-14), but Philippians 4:16 tells us that he was there long enough for financial help to come from Philippi. The NIV reads: '... for even when I was in Thessalonica, you sent me aid again and again when I was need.' On the surface, this would seem to imply that he was there for considerably longer than three weeks. But Leon Morris has pointed out in his commentary, that the Greek probably means, 'both when I was in Thessalonica and more than once in other places, you sent me aid again and again'.[1]

I think, on balance, the concern of the first letter points to a stay of very short length. Paul describes himself in 1 Thess-alonians 2:17 as 'torn away from them', and the word expresses the deep sorrow of bereavement, with his resultant anxiety to know whether they are going to endure through the trials and temptations they are facing. There is a deep concern in Paul as he writes the first letter just because he has been snatched away from them, after a very short time. He reassures them in 2:18: 'we wanted to come to you – certainly I, Paul, did, again and again – but Satan stopped us.' But while we don't know the exact duration of the time Paul stayed in Thessalonica, we do know the magnitude of the response. 'Some of the Jews were persuaded and joined Paul and Silas, as did a large number of God-fearing Greeks and not a few prominent women' (Acts 17:4).

This provides us with an interesting insight into the constitution of this young church from the very beginning. As Paul is obviously gospelling among God-fearers, it is significant that Luke tells us how he did it. 'He reasoned with them from the Scriptures, explaining and proving' and then proclaiming 'that the Christ had to suffer and rise' and that Jesus is the Christ (Acts 17:2-3). There is very strong Old Testament content and much for the mind, as well as the will, in this. Indeed, the appeal to the mind was always vital for Paul. He came not to generate an emotional response, but to persuade the minds of his hearers of the truth of his declaration, that Jesus is the Christ. We will need to bear that in mind when we come to look at his own account of what actually happened in Thessalonica.

The point to notice here is that it was extremely effective. The description of those who were his converts – some of the Jews and a large number (or a great multitude, it could be translated) of God-fearing Greeks, and not a few prominent women – indicates that the church was, by the standards of the Acts of the Apostles, a large body from the beginning. The God-fearing Greeks would have been attracted by the intellectual strength of Jewish monotheism. Many people in the pagan world found the morality of Judaism, with its clear ethical absolutes, a welcome alternative to the debauchery of classical mythology and religious ritual, so that it was not at all uncommon for Gentiles to become 'God-fearing'. But comparatively few became proselytes embracing Judaism totally, because of its ritual requirements and especially because of circumcision. Clearly, these people were fertile soil for the gospel seed, and Acts repeatedly tells us that they were among the first converts in many cities. Add to this no small number of the chief women, and you have a sizeable congregation of Gentiles, all converts from paganism via Judaism, together with a few believing Jews.

That is why verse 5 of Acts 17 is so significant, and provides us with the first important clue to solving the question of why Paul wrote 1 Thessalonians as he did: 'But the Jews were jealous.' It is not difficult to see why. Clearly, the synagogue elders had considerable numbers of Gentiles at varying stages of adherence to Judaism, as they had been quietly penetrating the pagan community. Now into this quiet backwater comes this heretical rabbi, who draws the converts away from the synagogue, with his erroneous messianic doctrine about the Christ having already come and about him being Jesus of Nazareth. Not surprisingly, when that happens, and you lose a large number of your Gentile adherents, your prestige levels in the city drop. After all, if you can take up Judaism so easily and then drop it equally quickly, perhaps there isn't that much in Judaism after all. We can see parallels in damage to the gospel by so-called converts who defect from the church.

So the Jews, in their jealousy, are determined that both Paul and his message must be discredited. He has to be opposed quickly and violently. Luke tells us that 'rent-a-mob' swings into action in order to lynch Paul and Silas, who, mercifully, are not at home when they besiege Jason's house. Instead, they make do with Jason and some other converts – notice the use of the word 'brothers' (v.6); it is the word that Paul is going to use in 1 Thessalonians again and again – and they arraign them before the city officials. And the *politarchs*, as Luke calls them (the correct local name for the magistrates in Thessalonica and one of those evidences of his historical accuracy), listen to the charge that is laid. It is a magnificent statement about the apostle's evangelism. 'These men who have caused trouble all over the world have now come here, and Jason has welcomed them into his house. They are all defying Caesar's decrees, saying that there is another king, one called Jesus.' What a splendid thing to be accused of!

The politarchs seem to have bound Jason and the others over to keep the peace (v. 9), but clearly the danger was intense and the situation volatile enough for Paul and Silas to be smuggled out at night (v. 10) and sent down the road to Berea. There, we are told, they had a more noble reception. 'They received the message with great eagerness and examined the Scriptures every day to see if what Paul said was true' (Acts 17:11).

Remember, we are in a world without phones or faxes, or even a postal service, and the founders of the church have gone. It is two days' travel down to Berea, and Paul, at least, is not going to be allowed to stay there very long. 'The brothers immediately sent Paul to the coast, but Silas and Timothy stayed at Berea' (Acts 17:14). So as he goes to the coast, possibly to go by ship to Athens, possibly to travel the coast road to the capital, two days by ship, nine or ten days on foot, he is going to be a very long way from his converts. The church in Thessalonica is on its own, and it faces a great test. There is another congregation ninety miles or so away in Philippi; and there will be a congregation in Berea when Silas and Timothy stay there and nurture it, but they won't stay for long; and anyway the Thessalonians won't know about its existence for some time. They are on their own; Paul has gone, suddenly wrenched from them. For him that will be almost intolerably painful, as he says in chapter 3 of his letter; but what about them?

The Jews who, until recently, were their friends and co-religionists are on to them. They were responsible for instigating the riot. The city authorities are certainly not inclined to look kindly on them, and some of their members – Jason and co – are on probation. In a situation like that, especially if it is only a month that Paul has had with them, wouldn't it be the easiest thing in the world for these young Christians to say, 'Well, let's call this whole thing off! Let's just admit that we have been temporarily hoodwinked by a very clever operator, a travelling salesman for religion, who actually took us in. Now let's just drift quietly back to the synagogue. OK, let's apologise, let's eat humble pie for a few weeks, and then forget that the whole episode happened at all.'? That is what you might very legitimately expect and by the time Paul reached Athens, it was what he feared. In that great intellectual and pagan centre, he wasn't run out of town, he was just ridiculed and largely ignored. Listen to Leon Morris: 'Small wonder, then, that when he got to Corinth he described himself as "in weakness and in fear and in much trembling".'[2] And that verse, 1 Corinthians 2:3, is rendered by J B Phillips in his paraphrase: 'I was feeling far from strong, I was nervous and rather shaky.' A very human Paul, clearly a very discouraged man at this point in his career. But it is precisely at this point in his career, in Corinth, that he writes 1 Thessalonians.

It is not easy to piece together all the background information. Silas and Timothy are left at Berea, Paul goes on to Athens, escorted by men from Berea, but then he is left alone as he waits for Silas and Timothy to join up with him as soon as possible – that is, presumably as soon as they consider the new church in Berea to be strongly enough grounded. Perhaps Paul insisted that they stay in Berea for the very reason that he was so concerned that they had all been bundled out of Thessalonica so unceremoniously. But the most likely scenario seems to be that they do catch up with him in Athens, some time after his famous Areopagus address. 1 Thessalonians 3:1-2 helps us to sort out the biographical information: 'So when we could stand it no longer, we thought it best to be left by ourselves in Athens. We sent Timothy, who is our brother and God's fellow-worker in spreading the gospel of Christ, to strengthen and encourage you in your faith.' The 'we', I think, implies Paul and Silas (they have all met up) sending Timothy now back to Thessalonica because the intensity of Paul's concern and anxiety is so great he can stand it no longer. And it is interesting, still in chapter 3 of 1 Thessalonians, that the plural becomes singular in verse 5: 'For this reason, when *I* could stand it no longer, I sent to find out about your faith.' That's probably because Paul also sent Silas back to Macedonia on another errand. But he is prepared to remain alone in Athens, and then to go on to Corinth alone, as Acts 18 tells us, where he lodged with Aquila and Priscilla. It is to there that Silas and Timothy come back from Macedonia to join him again (Acts 18:5). And it is Timothy's return which prompts this letter. So 1 Thessalonians 3:5-6, 'I was afraid that in some way the tempter might have tempted you and our efforts might have been useless. But Timothy has just now come to us from you and has brought good news about your faith and love.'

From Acts 18, then, we can conclude that Paul was in Corinth about 18 months before Gallio came as pro-consul (see Acts 18:11-12) and that he left soon after (Acts 18:18). We know from secular history that Gallio arrived in midsummer 51 AD, so it is likely that Paul arrived in Corinth early in 50 and left in the autumn of 51. If that is right, and it seems to me to hold up, then that would date the two letters to the Thessalonians, which are usually agreed to be separated by only a few months, in the years 50-51. This means that they are among the earliest letters of Paul, depending on whether Galatians pre-dates them or not. But either way, they were written less than twenty years after the crucifixion. They are especially insightful for us, therefore, into the earliest days of the church; into the ministry that founded it, the priorities that were to govern it, the pressures and problems that it faced, and into Paul's great concern for its continuance and well-being.

Relationship of 1 and 2 Thessalonians

Before we start to explore the text more closely and try to take a bird's-eye view of the first letter, it is worth considering the relationship of the two Thessalonian letters to each other, and how they work together.

There has been a good deal of scholarly argument about the order of the letters, and it has been suggested by a number of modern commentators that 1 Thessalonians was put first in the New Testament order only because of its greater length. On this theory, 2 Thessalonians was really the first letter, and therefore ought to be taken first in our considerations. The most recent exponent of the view that I have come across is Charles Wanamaker, in his commentary in the New International Greek Testament series, published in 1990, where he argues very strongly for the priority of 2 Thessalonians.[3] The issue, as he sees it, is that the problems about the Second Coming, and the idleness of some as they sit waiting for Christ's return, seem to be more acute in 2 Thessalonians, suggesting perhaps that it came first, and did its work in correcting those mistakes, explaining why there is less about them in 1 Thessalonians which would have followed on.

It is also argued that the reference to Paul's own signature, which you find in 2 Thessalonians 3:17 – 'I Paul, write this greeting in my own hand, which is the distinguishing mark in all my letters. This is how I write' – would be a more appropriate thing to say if you were writing a first letter to somebody. He is saying, 'This is my signature, this is my handwriting, so that you will know what a genuine letter from Paul looks like.

Against this it can be argued that most of Paul's letters to churches are 'first' letters, but none of them seems to have any such reference elsewhere. Moreover, there is also good internal reason in 2 Thessalonians for the signature. In 2 Thessalonians 2:2, Paul calls on them not 'to become easily unsettled or alarmed by some prophecy, report or letter supposed to have come from us, saying that the day of the Lord has already come'. That may well be the reason why he pens his own signature in his own handwriting so that they will know that it is a genuine letter from him.

It seems to me that the point to be made is that between the first and the second letter, the situation changed. Issues were clarified, while in some areas new problems developed and old problems deepened. In a perverse sort of way, maybe, it can be an encouragement to us to see that one letter from the apostle didn't automatically solve all the difficulties. We are sometimes tempted to think when we are in pastoral difficulties in our own churches, that if only we could wheel the apostle Paul in, that would be the automatic solution! But it doesn't seem to have worked like that in the New Testament. In 2 Thessalonians, Paul refers to a letter he has already written to them: '...brothers, stand firm and hold to the teachings we passed on to you, whether by word of mouth or by letter' (2 Thess. 2:15). So unless we are going to immerse ourselves in speculative theories about a lost letter, there seems to be perfectly adequate evidence for accepting the traditional order in the New Testament. Indeed the autobiographical material which is such a significant part of the first letter, is also much more suitable to a first letter, rather than to a follow-up letter.

Overview of 1 Thessalonians
For the last part of this chapter, we are now in a position to take an overview of 1 Thessalonians, to discover the terrain we are going to cover, and to begin to pick out some of the marker posts that I hope will become our familiar guide as we progress

through the letter. We are looking for the main themes, the main ideas, the big picture as to why the letter is here, what we might call 'the melodic line' or the 'theme tune'. That means we are going to be asking ourselves these two key questions all the time: What is the distinctive message of this letter that marks it out from all other New Testament Scripture? And, as we look at passages, What is the distinctive message of this passage and how does it fit the structure as a whole?

Questions like these are necessary, firstly, for our understanding of the text within its context, but I think they are absolutely vital also for our application of the text to our lives today. This whole area of application is one that many Christians find very difficult. We are good at drawing in applications from outside, discerning parallels and making comparisons, but we are not very good at finding the application of this particular passage and the thrust of what this passage teaches us. One of the things I have found in the last few years to be really helpful for application is getting the context right. If I can get the context right and see why it was written to people in their situation, that will very often open up the application for me in a way that is penetrating and persuasive. If we are cutting with the grain, our applications will be that much more obvious and clearly more directly drawn from Scripture, and when that happens our understanding will be much deeper and more significant. And the way to get there is by reading, reading and reading again; by careful observation of what it actually says, and by finding out the context as clearly as we can, so that by understanding the text in context we can move on to the application with confidence. We need to go digging for ourselves, and as we look for the big picture, the themes, the ideas, the issues and the questions, we get back into the Thessalonian context and into Paul's shoes as much as we can. That does require hard work but it is well worth it.

The initial greeting, 1:1, is unremarkable enough, but then 1:2-10 is one long sentence in the original. But we are interested in analysing content here, so 1:2-3, paragraphed for us by the

NIV, is a thanksgiving for three great Christian qualities, which Paul sees in the Thessalonian church – faith, love and hope – a familiar Pauline trio which he is going to use often in his later letters.

In 1:4-6, there are evidences of Christian reality, founded in the greatest security that any human being can know, which is the security that God has chosen you (v. 4). And there are two strands of evidence for this spiritual reality. The first, in verse 5, is the Holy Spirit's power, at work with deep conviction. So the verse reads: 'our gospel came to you not simply with words, but also with power, with the Holy Spirit and with deep conviction.' The other, in verse 6, is the Holy Spirit's joy experienced in receiving the gospel, in spite of the suffering it has brought: 'in spite of severe suffering, you welcomed the message with the joy given by the Holy Spirit'. How do we know God is at work in these people? We see the Holy Spirit's power and they have experienced the Holy Spirit's joy.

As a result, they have become a flagship church (1:7-10) – a model church. Everybody in both northern and southern Greece knows about their faith, and this gospel is being relayed all over the country and, indeed, further afield. 'Your faith in God has become known everywhere' (v. 8). Then verses 9-10 are a wonderfully compressed statement of the gospel, which they have welcomed, together with the authentic response that the power of the Holy Spirit has generated. So putting all that together, we can see how Paul's thanksgiving becomes for them a great assurance. That is the movement of the chapter. He is thanking God that they are authentic believers. They are a real church, because they have authentically received the authentic gospel. They have truly received the real message. The apostle Paul sees in them the marks of reality which they need to recognise as such, so what he is thanking God for becomes for them the source of an assurance in which they are to be grounded and to grow.

Now we need to ask the question: But why does he start like that? Why do they need that assurance? We move into chapter 2 and we find here that Paul begins the chapter by recalling his time with them when he was in Thessalonica. Verses 3-6 are largely a personal apologia, denying certain things, defending himself against certain attacks. For example, at verse 3, 'the appeal we make does not spring from error or impure motives, nor are we trying to trick you. On the contrary, we speak as men approved by God to be entrusted with the gospel. We are not trying to please men but God.' Verse 5: 'You know we never used flattery, nor did we put on a mask to cover up greed.' Verse 6: 'We were not looking for praise from men, not from you or anyone else.'

So far, it is largely negative. Paul runs through a whole catalogue of unworthy motives and unhelpful behaviour patterns, all of which he repudiates. He calls on them to remember the evidence they saw when he was with them. The phrase 'you know, brothers', at the beginning of the chapter, recurs many times in the letter, and more than once he solemnly calls God to witness that what he is saying is the sober truth. You see that in 2:5, 'God is our witness'; again in verse 10, 'You are witnesses, and so is God of how holy, righteous and blameless we were among you.' Clearly, then, for Paul, this is a very important matter. He is not just drawing a pen picture of what an authentic apostolic ministry looks like. You could study the passage that way, and it wouldn't be wrong, but it seems to me that he is defending himself from violent attack. That is what lies behind these verses, and when in verses 7-12 he moves to the positive, he reminds his readers of the models of faith and love which they saw in him – motherly care (v. 7), hard work (v. 9), holy living (v. 10), fatherly concern (v. 11). They have got to be recalled to the reality of what Paul's visit actually was like.

Then, as though to underline that, 2:13-16 returns to the theme of thanksgiving for their reception of the gospel. Clearly Paul's example affected their response to the message, and what he rejoices in is their authentic response to apostolic message and ministry. So they believe (v. 13) and as a result (v. 14) they suffer. That is an echo of the same process we have seen already in chapter 1, verses 5 and 6. They 'received the word with deep conviction' (1:5); 'you became imitators of us in severe suffering' (1:6). So the believing and the suffering go together.

In 2:14b-16, Paul's concern is to show them that they are not out on their own in this. What they have experienced of suffering comes from their own countrymen, as well as the Jews, and the Jewish persecution is not directed so much against them, as against Paul and his Gentile ministry. Indeed it is opposition to the Lord Jesus himself and therefore to God.

At this point, we need to start reflecting on both the provocation these Thessalonians are under, and on what is moving Paul to write. 2:17-3:10 is a long and deeply personal autobiographical passage, but again it is defensive, in the best sense of that word. There is a very strong protestation about the writer's love and concern for them all. There are some profound issues here about the relationship between the apostle and the church. He has an all-consuming desire to see them, because they, he says, are his 'joy and his crown'. That is why he sent Timothy to them as an agent of strength and encouragement, but also, 'to find out about your faith' (3:5). Could Paul's labour have been fruitless? Is it possible that everything he had been doing would prove to be empty? Have they really persevered? This explains why, when Timothy returns with a very positive report (3:6), Paul is ecstatic, 'Now we really live since you are standing firm in the Lord' (3:8). So, the section closes with his prayer requests for his return to them (3:11), for their love to grow (3:12), and for their holiness to increase (3:13).

Clearly, Paul's intention is to remind them of the reality of the gospel in which they have believed, in order to counteract what is going on in Thessalonica at the instigation of the jealous Jews. You see, Thessalonica is a fine church which has made a great beginning. It is a model church to all the other churches of Greece, both in its doctrine and in its lifestyle. It has become a flagship church, a church with a high profile, which is both an honour and a very great responsibility. Everybody is talking about the church in Thessalonica. Everybody knows that this church is large and has impressive people in it. Although it seems to have been founded so quickly, yet it appears to be a great triumph of the gospel. For that very reason, because of its high profile, the future of the gospel in Europe and the viability of Paul's own ministry hang on what happens to this flagship church in Thessalonica. And there are several potentially destructive pressure points.

Firstly, the Jews are not going to acquiesce in the defection of some of their most influential converts, so a determined slur campaign is being carried on against Paul, both as an individual and also against his message. There is also some persecution from their fellow-citizens in Thessalonica, who are pagan. When we come to chapter 5 we find that the weak are being tempted in the area of moral compromise, the timid are being unsettled, and there is an idle group of super-pious individuals, who are refusing to work and requiring the church to support them financially, so that they can devote themselves to the ministry of waiting for Jesus. This behaviour is generating internal disagreements over where the authority lies in the church, which chapter 5 is clearly addressing. There was probably not a little external criticism about the gullibility of a community which is prepared to support such loafers.

Paul is passionately committed to the well-being of his church; his whole life is devoted to this gospel ministry. They have, he says, become very dear to him, and he anticipates that his greatest joy in the last day will be their presence with him, blameless at the coming of the Lord Jesus. So it matters, now in time, that the Thessalonian church endures, and it matters for eternity. But the grave danger, the great fear that Paul has, is that in some way the tempter might tempt them, and that they may slip away through discouragement, or through pressure. That is why Paul gets out his pen to write, or to dictate to Silas this letter, which he wants to be read to all the brothers.

It is in the second part of the letter (chapters 4 and 5) where most of the teaching and encouragement come. This is the instruction and exhortation section. It is interesting that in later letters it is often the other way round, but here the teaching content comes in the second part. There is a little clue in 3:10, where Paul says, 'Night and day we pray most earnestly that we may see you again and supply what is lacking in your faith.' Timothy's report has been very positive, but clearly there are issues that need to be settled and deficiencies that need to be remedied and Paul does that in 4:1-2, with general introductory words that launch the second half of the letter – 'Finally, brothers, we instructed you how to live in order to please God, as in fact you are living. Now we ask you and urge you in the Lord Jesus to do this more and more. For you know what instructions we gave you by the authority of the Lord Jesus.'

So the practical teaching side of the letter is not a rebuke at all. The apostle is thrilled that they are living to please God, but he urges them to advance and increase in the same direction, to do this more and more. In this exhortation, the focus is on sexual purity (4:3-8), brotherly love (4:9-10), and responsible daily living (4:11-12). Then at 4:13 he begins to teach them what they do *not* currently know – 'Brothers we do not want you to be ignorant.' The first twelve verses are reminding them of what they need to do more and more – they already know that. But there is obviously some confusion about the *parousia* of the Lord Jesus and the state of those who have fallen asleep before he comes, so there is fresh instruction at this point. Lastly, in chapter 5, the implications of Christ's return are spelt out, as they are called on to be alert, self-controlled, children of the day. Once again it is the future perspective which conditions the lifestyle of the present.

The rest of chapter 5, from verse 12 on, is actually dealing with the relational needs in the Thessalonian church – the role of the leaders, how they are viewed, how its members are to get on with one another, what their priorities ought to be. Verses 16-22 is a very carefully and deliberately constructed little piece of prose, in a series of triplets put together. I don't think we can get away with just describing it as final instructions, because there is much more to it than that.

Then, 5:23-24 is the final prayer which sums up his concern for the church. It is for thorough-going Christlikeness, reiterating one of the great themes of the letter – the supremacy of Christ. Of course, if the Jews are on the attack, that is going to be the very area that they will go for. They will firstly try to rubbish Paul; then they will try to demolish his message. Paul's message was 'this Christ, that I declare to you, is called Jesus. He is the new King'. Obviously then, the attack is going to be on the person of Jesus, and the defence is going to be to convince and underscore the Christians' conviction that Jesus really is Lord. So although there are no classic Christological passages in 1 Thessalonians, the truth is all the way through the letter – the Lordship of Jesus. And it is here in the last prayer: 'May God himself, the God of peace, sanctify you through and through. May your whole spirit, soul and body be kept blameless at the coming of our Lord Jesus Christ.' That's where everything is moving. There is the focus of it all.

And then right at the end comes that amazing and glorious affirmation: 'The one who calls you is faithful and he will do it' (5:24). The last sentence of the letter prayer echoes the first – 'For we know, brothers, loved by God, that he has chosen you' (1:4). He has chosen you, he has called you, he will do it.

That is what the church needs to be assured of if it is going to persevere in the midst of all the pressures and suffering that it faces. What was true then is as true of the church in our generation as well, and I hope that even in this first brief sketch we have begun to see how much this letter has to say to us. We have the timid among us who are confused about their faith and who desperately need to be strengthened and encouraged. We have the faint-hearted who are very tempted to give way under the pressures of living as a Christian in a pagan environment. We may even have the idle, the super-spiritual, who are sitting back and letting it all drift by. We certainly face the pressures of a hostile world in terms of morality, in terms of our community life, and the greatest pressure of all to lose sight of the coming of the Lord Jesus and so to forget the far horizon which alone makes sense of the present. The message Paul wrote to first century Thessalonica could hardly be more appropriate or searching for the church at the end of the twentieth century.

2

A Faith That Works
1 Thessalonians 1:1-10

[1]Paul, Silas and Timothy, To the church of the Thessalonians in God the Father and the Lord Jesus Christ: Grace and peace to you.

[2]We always thank God for all of you, mentioning you in our prayers. [3]We continually remember before our God and Father your work produced by faith, your labour prompted by love, and your endurance inspired by hope in our Lord Jesus Christ.

[4]For we know, brothers loved by God, that he has chosen you, [5]because our gospel came to you not simply with words, but also with power, with the Holy Spirit and with deep conviction. You know how we lived among you for your sake. [6]You became imitators of us and of the Lord; in spite of severe suffering, you welcomed the message with the joy given by the Holy Spirit. [7]And so you became a model to all the believers in Macedonia and Achaia. [8]The Lord's message rang out from you not only in Macedonia and Achaia – your faith in God has become known everywhere. Therefore we do not need to say anything about it, [9]for they themselves report what kind of reception you gave us. They tell how you turned to God from idols to serve the living and true God, [10]and to wait for his Son from heaven, whom he raised from the dead – Jesus, who rescues us from the coming wrath (1 Thess. 1:1-10).

Everything in this stimulating chapter, which is in fact one long sentence, is dependent on the main verb at the start of verse 2 – 'we give thanks'. The letter is generated by the enormously good news that Timothy has brought of the continuing faith and love of the Thessalonian believers. So it is not surprising that its assurances, which actually contain a great deal of teaching content, are expressed in the context of thanksgiving.

The evidences and qualities of the Thessalonian believers, for which Paul thanks God, are the very confirmations which they need to identify in order to assure them that they really are on track. It is not only in the twentieth century, it must be in every century and in every group of Christian people, that the greatest human quest is for spiritual reality. Of course, that is what we all want, and that is what people, whether religious or not, are chasing all the time. Everyone is looking for reality. But the great issue is how are we to discern the true from the spurious. How are we to discern reality and preserve it when we find it? The Thessalonian church was undoubtedly under pressure from the Jews to concede that they had got the wrong message, and that they had begun to follow the wrong messenger. And that has a contemporary ring about it, doesn't it?

Verse 3 is the germ of Paul's answer, as well as providing an agenda for the whole letter. Rather as Acts 1:8 provides the agenda or title page for that great book, with the gospel spreading from Jerusalem through Judea and Samaria to the ends of the earth (Rome in chapter 28), so 1 Thessalonians 1:3 is a title page for this letter. Faith, love and hope are three great Christian distinctives to which Paul is going to return over and over again. And not only Paul, but Peter and the writer to the Hebrews refer to these essential ingredients of orthodox Christianity.*

The structure of verse 3 is very simple and uncluttered. It reads literally: 'your work of faith, your labour of love, your endurance of hope.' The word 'your' is placed in a position of emphasis and Ernest Best, in his commentary, suggests that it

---

* For example, Ephesians 1:15; Colossians 1:4, 23; 2 Thessalonians 1:3; Philemon 5; Hebrews 10:22-24; 1 Peter: 1:8, 22; 2 Peter 1:5-7.

probably governs each of the six main words – *your* faith that
works, *your* love that labours, *your* endurance inspired by hope,
or your hope that endures.[1] The NIV provides a very felicitous
translation in terms of its public reading, but we do need to
recognise that it has introduced certain verbs into verse 3.
'Produced', 'prompted' and 'inspired' are not there in the
original. Undoubtedly this has been done to make the relationship
between the pairs of words – work/faith, labour/love, endurance/
hope – clear and plain. That is very helpful for us, provided as
English readers we are not trapped into expounding the additional
vocabulary, which isn't actually there. So a sermon that majors
on prompting and inspiring owes more to the NIV translators
than to Paul. But the translation does make clear that the work,
the labour and the endurance stem from and are the expression
of the faith, the love and the hope. The emphasis is on the virtues
themselves and the proof of their presence in the activity of the
believers.

If we wanted to sum up the thrust of verse 3, it would be: real
faith works, real love labours, real hope perseveres, and because
all these things are seen in your life then there is every evidence
that you are real Christians. Praise God!

Now that introduces us to a very important principle which
is as vital for us to grasp as it was for the Thessalonians. Indeed,
it becomes the theme tune of chapter 1. Let me put it this way:
faith obviously must have objective content, and verses 9 and
10 at the end of the chapter will make abundantly clear what
that content is. This is the faith that works. It is based on God's
intervention in Christ Jesus (v. 10) who comes on a great rescue
mission and who procures our salvation through his death and
resurrection. So Christian faith has an objective correlative. There
is a reality in time and space, in which it trusts and on which it
stands. And we must always affirm that when we are talking
about faith. So many people think that faith is just a process of
trying to come to some sort of internal peace through a personal
belief system, which can be any system and any belief. It was
Robert Louis Stevenson who said, 'It is better to travel hopefully

than to arrive.' That sort of idea about faith is very common today. It is the idea that the journey is all important; it is the experience of travelling that is the real significance. But Paul is saying, 'No; it is the destination that gives the journey any sort of significance at all.' Faith must have an objective reality, or else it is merely wishful thinking.

Love is the relationship between God and his people, restored through Jesus the Rescuer. It is expressed in the Church in the quality of relationships between those who have been rescued.

Hope is the expectation of the completion of that great work, when the Rescuer returns, as Lord and King to wind up human history, to bring in his everlasting kingdom, and to rescue us from the wrath that will be revealed (v. 10).

Of course it is right and good for us to talk about faith, love and hope in those ways. It is possible for us to take each of these qualities, to articulate, describe and explain them, and to accept them as intellectually credible and true. That is what Paul was doing in the synagogue at Thessalonica as he explained, reasoned and proved from the Scriptures that Jesus had to die and rise, and that Jesus is the Christ. But the significant thing is this, and I think it is very important for understanding this chapter: Paul does not point to the objective content *alone* as the evidence of spiritual reality. That content is absolutely vital and without it Christianity would not be Christianity, but simply to embrace that content intellectually, or even hold on to it tenaciously as a doctrinal position, is not where Paul puts his emphasis. What he remembers with thankfulness is the active proof, externally, of the inward reality. The work, the labour and the endurance are the proofs of the reality.

I am labouring this a little because I think we Christians have become very accustomed to the polarisation of dogma and experience, which so often and so fatally expresses itself in an antipathy between head and heart, truth and love, even Word and Spirit. For many years now we have suffered in evangelical circles in this country from this antipathy which divides and polarises. But the New Testament always binds both together, and both are needed if we are to have biblical assurance. The reason isn't really so difficult to see. It is that God's self-revelation in Scripture is not just propositional. It is that, and the propositional revelation is non-negotiable, but it is not just propositional, it is also relational. That's the way Scripture works. So my faith is not just belief in a creed, it is trust in a person whose nature and activity the creed explains and describes. And that sort of faith – trust in a person – will always express itself in activity; every relationship does.

Similarly, Christian love (agape) is experienced in relationship of a deeply personal kind with that person – the living God – and then with our neighbour. And that sort of love must always express itself. True love always does. It is not just a word, it must be expressed in activity, and in this context, the reality of our love for God and for our fellow human beings can be seen in the way we live.

Even our hope is personal. The end of verse 3 says that it is 'hope in our Lord Jesus Christ'. Again, it is possible to realise that our hope is the hope of heaven, and of course that's right, but Jesus is the end and goal of everything. That sort of hope perseveres and holds up under all sorts of trials and tests. So, we must hold these two modes of reality together in all our teaching and in all our assessment of Christian experience and living. We have to affirm that our Christian experience is important. Christian reality is a relationship with our God and Father, in and through our Lord Jesus Christ. It is a relationship we can enter into only as we respond in faith to the propositional self-revelation of God in Scripture. But it is a relationship. And those of us who are strong on propositional truth must never be boxed into a corner, where because of a false polarity we are almost forced to deny the experiential ingredient. Paul is binding them both together, inextricably, as the apostles always do. You cannot learn theology as you might learn algebra. It is about a relationship with God. That is what is at the heart of his assurance for them, and the heart of our instruction in this letter. But it is very hard for us to get that right in our contemporary situation.

I remember, a few years ago, a news item in the press, reporting on the religious education debate that was going on in the House of Commons, and the government minister was quoting from various recent letters that had been received on the subject. He had some letters that had been sent to Church House, Westminster, and he read one which, he said, was not untypical of the sort of approach to religious education that is all too common in many schools. The letter was very brief, it said: 'Dear sir, This term in RE we are doing God. Please send full details and pamphlets.' In a culture like that, it is not surprising that people feel that either Christianity is so theoretical as not to impinge on them, or else are so desperate for experience that they will embrace anything.

Paul's appeal here is to the irrefutable evidence of life, but that is only explicable in terms of the reality of belief. That is the kingpin of what he is saying in this chapter. The objective realities prove themselves to be genuine in the revolution of lifestyle that they produce, as nothing else can. So while Dr. Martyn Lloyd-Jones used to say, I think quite rightly, that orthodoxy can never be dead orthodoxy, because orthodoxy is always alive as the truth of God is, nevertheless we have to admit that sometimes it can be very dry and detached orthodoxy and that God's 'frozen people' are not part of Paul's agenda for the Thessalonians, or for us.

Let us see, now, how the two strands are woven closer together as the chapter develops. Many times in this letter, Paul will say 'you know, brothers...' but here he begins, '*we* know, brothers...' (v. 4). In fact it is a present participle that depends on the 'we give thanks...'. Tracing the structure from verse 2, it runs we give thanks, mentioning (v. 2), remembering (v. 3), knowing (v. 4). He wants them to share the assurances and convictions he has about them, because they are all grounded in God's electing grace. Verse 4: 'knowing, brothers loved by God, that he has chosen you.' So the qualities of verse 3 are proof not just that the gospel works. Many philosophies and beliefs may 'work', in all sorts of different ways. Verse 3 is the proof that

God is working, that they themselves are evidence of God's
love and mercy at work in the wonder of their salvation, and
there can be no reality more ultimate or more dependable than
the fact that God has chosen you. For Paul, then, the evidence
and proof of our election is in both our current believing correctly
and our faithful living. It was their eager response to the gospel
which first convinced him that God was at work, and Timothy's
report has wonderfully confirmed that. That is why Paul doesn't
thank the Thessalonians; he thanks God. His choice is the
outworking of his love, but we must never forget that the New
Testament emphasis is on election to the service of God, hence
the emphasis on work and labour in verse 3, and the verb at the
end of verse 9, 'to serve the living and true God'. We cannot
predict where God's love will be active, choosing men and
women for faith and love and hope, but we can see the evidences
of that reality, which should both encourage and challenge us.

Paul now spells this out in Thessalonian terms. There are
two strands of evidence, each of which exhibits this double-
sided Christian reality of truth and experience. In the first strand,
he reminds them of how they received the gospel. 'Our gospel
came to you not simply with words, but also with power, with
the Holy Spirit and with deep conviction' (v.5). Notice, first of
all, that the gospel has to come with words. Its truth content has
to be articulated, and that is important to stress because it means
that the choosing grace of God operates through the declaration
of the good news. Every gospel preacher believes that. So we
need to keep that clearly in view as a corrective to the idea that
Christianity is caught, rather than taught, or that 'presence
evangelism' is sufficient, or that the precision of content doesn't
really matter so long as you feel the love of Jesus.

If we go that way, we shall lose the heart of our message and
end up with a 'gospel' which is largely lacking content and which
will not produce Christian disciples. We shall be like the fisher-
man who, when asked how many he caught, said that he hadn't
actually caught any fish, but he thought he might have influenced
quite a large number! No, the gospel has to come in words, yet

not simply in words. That is literally not in words alone. You see, this was the controversy in Thessalonica. Words were cheap and all the travelling salesmen on the religious circuit in the ancient world would be very adept at using them. We saw in Acts 17 how Paul reasoned, explained, proved and persuaded his synagogue hearers, but what he is telling us is that it was not his speech that did the job. There was another supernatural ingredient at work – the power of the Holy Spirit.

On a visit to the United States, I found it fascinating to watch the religious channels and the shopping channels on television back-to-back. As you graze between them, you are struck by how similar their methods, their style and even their vocabulary are. You see, in terms of words there is no real difference. One is selling Christianity and the other is selling jewellery, clothing or whatever it may be. There is no great difference in terms of the words. If there is any difference between them, it is going to be because there is the power of the Holy Spirit at work when the gospel is really preached. Paul's critics are saying that he is only a wordsmith, just another huckster, a religious salesman. But the apostle's defence is that what has happened in Thessalonica is evidence of divine power at work. So the church is not to be influenced, or subverted, by these smears.

But there is some discussion about where the 'power and deep conviction' of the Holy Spirit are to be located. Is he talking about it in the preacher or in the hearers when he says, 'our gospel came to you with power, with the Holy Spirit and with deep conviction'? Is he saying that is how you heard it or that is how I preached it? Well, perhaps the answer is both, but I think the emphasis in the context is on their reception of it. I am sure he did preach it with deep conviction, but what he is stressing is their joyful reception of the gospel, because at this point Paul is wanting to encourage them to rejoice in the genuineness of their experience, rather than the validity of his ministry. He wants them to know that he is a true apostle and that he was preaching the true word, but here he is saying to them that the fact that the gospel has been received by them in this way is evidence of the

Holy Spirit at work. So that's a very important lesson. How do you know the gospel of Christ is more than human words? Because the power of the Holy Spirit is seen in the deep conviction produced in the hearers.

We also need to see the significance of that word 'conviction' at the end of the sentence. It is a word that really means 'assurance', rather than 'conviction' in the sense of conviction of sin. A couple of other references where it is used, one by Paul and one in Hebrews, demonstrate this. In Colossians 2:2, Paul says: 'My purpose is that they may be encouraged in heart and united in love, so that they may have the full riches of complete understanding, in order that they may know the mystery of God.' So the assurance or conviction there is the complete understanding, which comprehends and then believes. Or, in a famous passage in Hebrews, it is used again. 'We want each of you to show this same diligence to the very end, in order to make your hope sure' (Heb. 6:11), and in Hebrews 10:22, it is translated 'full assurance of faith'. It is the same word translated in those three different ways in three different contexts: complete understanding, diligence to the end, full assurance of faith. That is what the Holy Spirit produced in them – the assurance that this was true and it was to be held on to.

So what do we have here in 1 Thessalonians 1:5? Surely an important statement about the Holy Spirit as the agent of power, who produces a personal assurance in the hearers of the gospel, that these things are indeed true, that they are loved of God, chosen by him, that Jesus is the Lord from heaven, and that he is the Rescuer from the coming wrath. That inner persuasion of the gospel's reality is deeper and more pervasive than any appeal to external signs or power displays. In fact, the external signs are in the lifestyle of those who have become deeply convinced about the gospel's truth.

This must be the right emphasis because if you go to the next part of verse 5, you have the sentence: 'You know how we lived among you for your sake.' For reasons best known to themselves, the NIV translators have omitted the very significant link-word, *kathos* – 'just as', 'even as' – which makes the link back with what he has just said. Paul is stressing the mutual assurance and encouragement implicit in this. He says at the end of verse 5, the fact that we lived authentic gospel lives among you – and chapter 2 will expound what that means – helped to convince you of the truth of our words. And now we, in turn, are convinced about the reality of your faith, because we see that this gospel has similarly changed you deeply, too. 'You know how we lived among you for your sake' (v.5), 'You became imitators of us and of the Lord' (v.6).

He appeals to what they already know. It is the first time he says, 'you know' and this phrase is going to occur a good deal throughout the letter. '*You know*, brothers, our visit wasn't a failure' (2:1). 'With the help of our God, as *you know*, we dared to tell you his gospel' (2:2). '*You know* we never used flattery' (2:5). '*You know* that we dealt with each of you as a father deals with his children' (2:11). '*You know* quite well that we were destined for trials' (3:3). 'It has turned out that way, as *you well know*' (3:4). '*You know* what instructions we gave you by the authority of the Lord Jesus' (4:2). '*You know* very well that the day of the Lord will come like a thief in the night' (5:2). Why this emphasis? As you study the references, you find that they are all a blend of propositional revelation and personal experience. Paul's point is that we are not to be easily unsettled from these anchor-points of Christian reality. Both are vital. There will always be false teachers who will propound error in many attractive ways, but they cannot counterfeit the power of the Holy Spirit in deep conviction of assurance. Nor can they counterfeit the joy of the Holy Spirit (which he focuses on in verse 6), 'in spite of severe suffering'.

Similarly, there will always be spurious experiences on offer which will produce all sorts of personal intensity, emotional highs, colly-wobbles, warm fuzzies, cold water down the spine, you name it! These are generated not by the gospel but by human psychological mechanisms and sometimes by manipulative techniques. How do we know? Because they don't produce imitators of the Lord. That's the point in verse 6. Paul doesn't want the Thessalonian Christians to give up their properly grounded assurance under assaults from either end of the spectrum, and neither should we.

Marks of gospel reality

What is the mark of gospel reality? It is that believers go on gladly receiving the word in spite of the severe suffering that it will inevitably bring. That is indisputable evidence of the Holy Spirit at work. So that's the gospel lifestyle Paul identifies as real Christianity. The assurance is not that they are living glorious lives of constant victory, floating above all the normal pressures of the world. The assurance in verse 6 is that they go on welcoming the message and relaying it with the joy which God gives them, in the midst of the severe suffering which that ministry inevitably causes. That is uniquely Christian. That is imitating the Lord – 'who for the joy that was set before him, endured the cross, scorning its shame' (Heb. 12:2). That is imitating the apostles – 'rejoicing because they had been counted worthy of suffering disgrace for the Name' (Acts 5:41). So you became imitators of us and of the Lord. There is the unassailable proof of God's electing love. The Holy Spirit is at work in power when the truth of the gospel is burned into the minds and hearts of the hearers, with deep assurance, for only the Holy Spirit can do that. Secondly, the Holy Spirit is at work in power when he brings joy to those believers to go on embracing, believing and living God's word whatever the personal cost may be. And, as verse 7 puts it, that is model New Testament Christianity.

It is also model twentieth century Christianity! We need ourselves to be assured of that, and we need to be totally unembarrassed and unashamed of it, since there are so many alternative versions of the Christian faith on offer today. We need to have a biblical standard by which to assess things and it is this. The mark of the true gospel is that it produces faith that works, love that labours, and hope that endures, and the mark of all spiritual reality is that it moves towards those goals. If some new, so-called spiritual, reality actually pulls people away from those goals it is to be rejected. If it rubbishes the work of the gospel that has been going on in the church, and people start to say, 'Well, it is this new thing that we need, and that old gospel preaching was all right for a while, but there is something beyond it to which we are moving on', you can be very sure that the new thing is not the work of the Holy Spirit. Here we see what the Holy Spirit actually produces. We must not be ashamed or embarrassed to state these things. The Bible does not leave us without standards of judgment. It shows us the criteria which have to be applied to our own spirituality and to every other spirituality. So, the first way in which Paul assures the Thessalonians of the reality of God in their lives – although the Jews are saying they have followed the wrong man and the wrong message – is that he reminds them of how they received the gospel and of how that gospel has worked in them.

Secondly, Paul turns to the other great mark of reality, for which he gives thanks (vv. 7 and 8). He reminds them of how they relayed the gospel. First, how they received it; then how they relayed it. 'And so you became a model to all the believers in [Greece]. The Lord's message rang out from you not only in Macedonia and Achaia' – that's the northern province and the southern province – 'your faith in God has become known everywhere. Therefore we do not need to say anything about it.' Now again, the NIV omits a rather important link-word at the beginning of verse 8, the word 'for'. 'For the Lord's message rang out from you', which shows us that verse 8 is the evidence for verse 7. Also the phrase 'from you' is in the emphatic position at the start of the clause. 'For *from you* the Lord's message rang out.' That's why you are a flagship church. That's why you are a model, because the word of the Lord has sounded out from Thessalonica, throughout the whole of Greece and even further afield.

Notice again that the important thing is how the objective truth is linked with the personal lifestyle. For this message, which obviously is the propositional truth of the gospel, has been incarnated in their lives. That's why he says, 'The Lord's message rang out from you', and then look at the middle of verse 8: 'your faith in God has become known everywhere' – literally, your faith towards God is what everybody has come to know about. Do you see how he puts the two very clearly together? Christians have been encouraged, and others have been encouraged to become Christians. They are a model, a flagship church, because they have not only got the truth right, but their faith in that truth is demonstrated in their lifestyle.

There is a lot here, both directly and by implication, for us in the contemporary church. It is a great peril to try and correct one imbalance by swinging the pendulum too far in the opposite direction. Yet so often by over-reacting we end up with an equally distorted position. I have been involved in Christian ministry for nearly thirty years and during that time I have watched the evangelical pendulum swinging, often violently, between the objective and the subjective, between what we might call the 'cerebral' or 'intellectual' and the 'intuitive' or 'emotional', with each new action tending to produce an equal and opposite reaction. The question that we have so often forgotten to ask ourselves is where the biblical perpendicular lies. For you never correct the swing of the pendulum by pushing it too far in the opposite direction; you just get a swing back.

Paul is not pleading for balance. That is a notoriously subjective category. One man's balance is another man's extremism, and balance will always tend towards compromise to lowest common denominator Christianity, to blandness, ultimately to stagnation. But the biblical perpendicular is quite another concept. Indeed, to many people the biblical perpendicular will itself appear totally unbalanced. But the Bible is the only reference point that is truly objective, because it is the eternal, unchanging revelation of the mind of God. That is why it is the perpendicular – inspired, inerrant and sufficient. And what this chapter challenges me to ask is whether I am following Paul's biblical perpendicular in seeing that both truth and lifestyle are essential ingredients of New Testament

Christianity, and indeed together constitute the proof that the gospel is reality. For many of us the danger is that we may be quite strong on the content of the Lord's message, probably a good deal stronger than we are on our faith in God being known everywhere, and yet we know from experience that it is the changed lifestyle that most frequently draws people to hear gospel proclamation. That's what happens in revival, isn't it? It explains why conviction and deep repentance among God's people always precede times of great fruitfulness in gospel preaching, and what draws the crowds, under the sovereign work of the Holy Spirit, is that the Christians' faith in God has become widely known.

So Paul didn't have to send out prayer letters boasting about how successful his mission to Thessalonica had been. Everybody was talking about the changed lives of these pagans and God-fearers and their faithful commitment to Christ along with their love and hope, and the fact that they kept on with this gospel in spite of the enormous troubles and trials it brought them. So, if it is true that the world needs fewer salesmen of the gospel and more free samples, is that emphasis reflected in ourselves and our gospel work? Have we, as gospel people, been content simply with words? They may be true, faithful, God-honouring words, but what have the words produced? What kind of reception have they been given? That is where the mark of reality is seen, and that is what we should expect to happen. This will not send us on a quest for some external success mechanism, or to assess our ministries by numbers or secular criteria, but every time we see in the grace of God an individual turn from idols to serve the living and the true God, that is the proof of the Holy Spirit at work, there is the demonstration of spiritual reality. Don't be moved from it.

Serving the true and living God

The chapter ends with a marvellous statement both of the message and the response that it generated in Thessalonica. It is not a comprehensive statement of the gospel, because it is strongly Thessalonian in its orientation. Paul is driving home his point, but I think it is a wonderfully distilled and focused summary of what he preached and what happened as a result, which is designed to produce great assurance. These words are written to assure them that they really are on track, that they have had a real messenger from God, preaching the real message of God, and what they have received is the real gospel. Here is the evidence and proof. 'They tell how you turned to God from idols to serve the living and true God, and to wait for his Son from heaven, whom he raised from the dead – Jesus, who rescues us from the coming wrath' (vv. 9-10).

Having studied the chapter, we are not surprised to find here the same wonderful blend of objective truth and personal lifestyle response. The nouns are all about objective truth – the living and true God, his Son from heaven, Jesus the Rescuer. The verbs are all about personal response – turn, serve, wait. That's the message they welcomed and that's how they welcomed it. And this is authentic, apostolic Christianity, in both content and in response. Here is the powerful work of the Holy Spirit.

What is the content? It is the living and true God, as opposed to idols. To many a modern mind that sounds surprisingly objective, and 'out there', remote even. Does it mean that Paul didn't start where the people were, as we are always being told we must? I want to answer that by saying 'yes' and 'no'. He clearly related all that he said to where they were, because they were worshipping idols, many of them, and his purpose in proclaiming the true God to them was to turn them. So there is no idea here of an academic theological detachment, but neither did he begin with their felt needs; he proclaimed God. If it is true that God has made us for himself and our hearts will always be restless till they find their rest in him, then to know the living and true God is our greatest human need. However, the Bible is a book that starts with God, rather than me, and presents a God-centred universe, rather than a me-centred microcosm. It is not hesitant to address me head-on, in terms of divine revelation, rather than in terms of personal need. You can see Paul do that over and over again in his recorded speeches and sermons. He preaches God. In his book, *The Supremacy of God in Preaching,* John Piper reminds us of Cotton Mather, one of the Puritan preachers who ministered in New England three hundred years ago, who reminded himself and his hearers that the great design and intention of the office of a Christian preacher [is] to restore the throne and dominion of God in the souls of men.[2] That is always the primary task of all Christian ministers, because idolatry is always the problem. Idolatry exercises a powerfully magnetic attraction on every human being because it seems to be the very way to escape our creature-hood. From Genesis 3 onwards, the desire is the same: you will be like God, knowing good and evil. Be your own god. That is why idols are so powerful. It does not matter what you use to be the focus of your worship – it can be primitive lumps of wood or stone, or highly sophisticated technological systems or philosophical theories, but idolatry will always dethrone God and always offer the attraction of worshipping the creature, ultimately ourselves, rather than the Creator.

There is only one counter-force that is strong enough to overcome the magnetic pull of idolatry in the human heart, and that is the knowledge of the living and the true God. When I realise and understand who this God is, and when that becomes the dominant reality in my life, then I shall turn from idols, but not until then. That sort of change can never be produced by human ability, only by divine power.

To know that God is alive and real, that idols are non-entities, vain and lifeless, that is the basis of the turning, and that was the appeal of God to his old covenant people all the way through Israel's history. It is the first commandment – no gods beside me. It is the second commandment – no idols to bow down to or to worship. But the awful irony is that even while Moses was on the mountain receiving that law, the people constructed the golden calf for the very purpose of bowing down to it and sacrificing to it (Exod. 32:1-6). It is not surprising then that when God renews his revelation to Moses in Exodus 34, that it is

precisely in these terms, that he is the living and real God. So, in
Exodus 34:6, the Lord proclaims his name: 'Yahweh, Yahweh,
the compassionate and gracious God, slow to anger, abounding
in love and faithfulness, maintaining love to thousands, and
forgiving wickedness, rebellion and sin. Yet he does not leave
the guilty unpunished.' The reality of Yahweh is seen in his
character and his actions. But the only proof that we really do
know and believe in the living and true God is that we serve
him. To say that I believe in the God of the Bible, without then
submitting myself to him as his *doulos*, his slave, is to lie and to
deceive myself. How could my relationship to such a God be
anything other than service? But that's the struggle, isn't it? All
the time the idols are in charge, I can worship me, I can please
myself. That is their attraction. The change conversion produces
is that I do not only turn, but I *serve*. Faith leads me to turn, love
leads me to serve, and hope leads me to 'wait for his Son from
heaven, whom he raised from the dead'. What a powerful
corrective that is. I wonder whether many Christians would
habitually describe the Christian life as serving and waiting, but
that is Paul's confirmation of reality. Once God becomes the
central reference point, then eternity, rather than time, becomes
the dominant dimension.

So, it is the future hope that controls verse 10, and what a
rich verse it is! The link between verses 9 and 10 is that I can
only truly come to know the living and true God through his
Son, so the focus shifts to Jesus. And because the perspective is
future, it shifts to Jesus as the Rescuer from the coming wrath.
The compression of verses 9-10 is masterly. When you start to
unpack it, it is amazing what is squeezed in there. Jesus is the
Rescuer, the Saviour, as his name indicates. Notice how the
verses teach us that he is the Son of the living and true God, that
is, the very life of God is within him. He is nothing less than the
living and true God incarnate. In that human body he died, and
in that body he was buried and raised from the dead. He ascended
to heaven where he now lives and reigns. And from there, the
eternally-alive Jesus will return at the end of all things to be

seen to be the Rescuer from the wrath of God, which is coming on rebellious humanity. It is all there in verses 9 and 10. So our waiting is not inactive; it is characterised by serving. This Christian lifestyle, in the present, is generated by the future realities of faith and hope, which are not yet ours.

This, then, is the spectacular change to which Paul wants to draw our attention. To have turned from idols, to be serving the unseen but living and true God, and to be waiting for his Son from heaven, is a change of immense proportions which is only attributable to the power of the Holy Spirit at work through the authentic message of the apostolic messengers. That is why he can say in 2:1: 'You know, brothers, that our visit to you was not a failure.'

Verses 9 and 10 are actually two three-line stanzas, or statements, each containing a past, present, and future reference and each pulling the objective and the personal together. They unite together the themes of the chapter. The Jesus who is the Son of God is the Jesus who died and was raised, past tense; who now is in heaven, present tense; and who will rescue his people from wrath when he comes, future tense. There is the objective reality of the faith. Meanwhile, Christians, in terms of the personal response, are people who have turned from idols to the living and true God, past tense; who are serving that God, present tense; and who will wait for that full salvation until Christ is revealed. That is how their faith works, their love labours, and their hope endures. And those, Paul says, are the marks of reality, which he discerns in the Thessalonian church, which cause him to give thanks to God, and which others discern in the Thessalonian church too. As a result, they should have every assurance that what has happened to them is God's work, that they are experiencing spiritual reality now, and that the full salvation will be theirs in the last day. When the Jews come with their message, 'You've got it all wrong; come back to the synagogue', that is the answer they are to give them. That is the rejoicing that they and Paul and every Christian already have in the reality of God's electing love. The gospel has come with the power of the Holy Spirit to transform our lives and to keep us pressing on, believing it and relaying it to a lost world, which is coming to God's judgment seat.

3

A Love that Labours (1)
1 Thessalonians 2:1-16

You know, brothers, that our visit to you was not a failure. [2]We had previously suffered and been insulted in Philippi, as you know, but with the help of our God we dared to tell you his gospel in spite of strong opposition. [3]For the appeal we make does not spring from error or impure motives, nor are we trying to trick you. [4]On the contrary, we speak as men approved by God to be entrusted with the gospel. We are not trying to please men but God, who tests our hearts. [5]You know we never used flattery, nor did we put on a mask to cover up greed – God is our witness. [6]We were not looking for praise from men, not from you or anyone else.

As apostles of Christ we could have been a burden to you, [7]but we were gentle among you, like a mother caring for her little children. [8]We loved you so much that we were delighted to share with you not only the gospel of God but our lives as well, because you had become so dear to us. [9]Surely you remember, brothers, our toil and hardship; we worked night and day in order not to be a burden to anyone while we preached the gospel of God to you.

[10]You are witnesses, and so is God, of how holy, righteous and blameless we were among you who believed. [11]For you know that we dealt with each of you as a father deals with his own children, [12]encouraging, comforting and urging you to live lives worthy of God, who calls you into his kingdom and glory.

[13]And we also thank God continually because, when you received the word of God, which you heard from us, you accepted it not as the word of men, but as it actually is, the word of God, which is at work in you who believe. [14]For you, brothers, became imitators of God's churches in Judea, which are in Christ Jesus: You suffered from your own countrymen the same things those churches suffered from the Jews, [15]who killed the Lord Jesus and the prophets and also drove us out. They displease God and are hostile to all men [16]in their effort to keep us from speaking to the Gentiles so that they may be saved. In this way they always heap up their sins to the limit. The wrath of God has come upon them at last (1 Thess. 2:1-16).

The opening verse of chapter 2 clearly marks the transition from the thanksgiving section to what we might call the body of the letter. What follows could well be called the heart-beat of the letter, because the whole of this section is dealing with Paul himself and the ministry God has given him. He continues to refute the criticisms that were being levelled at him by the 'jealous Jews' of Thessalonica, by explaining what his ministry was and why he did it that way. Its value to us lies in its apostolic definition of what authentic gospel ministry is all about and in the picture that is painted of an authentic gospel minister.

Several modern commentators have pointed out that Paul is using a classical rhetorical style, which was culturally attuned to first century Greek city-life. Its structure would therefore be more readily accessible to them than it is to us, in a different culture. Of course this point could be made about all biblical revelation. God's unchanging universal truth is always presented through the particularity of an individual writer, at a particular point in history, communicating to his own generation, in the language and thought forms with which they are familiar. It is this principle which comes to its fullest development in what has been called the 'scandal' of the incarnation. When the Word became flesh, it was in a particular man who lived at a particular time and place, but whose words and works have universal and eternal meaning. Paul was himself very much a first century man, and in terms of his style of writing and the way in which he presented material, he is obviously using what would be familiar to his first century Greek readers. But F. F. Bruce in his commentary makes the important point that there is nothing merely formal or stylistic about it.[1] We are not following material in which rhetorical artifice is the dominating concern. Often the language is very intense, quite broken, because there is a good deal of emotional fervour in what Paul is saying. The great apostle is defending the purity of his motives and the integrity of his behaviour, which makes this one of the most powerful and most moving of all the personal passages in his writings.

The activity of the missionaries and the response of the

Thessalonians are the two major strands of thought here in this unit. In verses 1-12, the focus is on Paul's gospel activity, while in verses 13-16 it is the Thessalonians' response which is examined. And just as in chapter 1, the truth and the reality of the message was confirmed by the changed lifestyle of those who received it, so now Paul focuses on confirming the reality of the message by calling as witness the personal integrity of the messenger, the one who proclaimed it. There can be no separation between the two; the message must be realised in the messenger, and that, says Paul, is precisely what happened.

It is important that we do not lose the particularity of the passage for the Thessalonians, facing all sorts of hostile attacks on their faith and their apostle. Indeed, the better we understand what it meant for them, the more readily we shall understand why the Holy Spirit has preserved the letter for us and the continuing good of the church in every generation. The applications become increasingly pertinent and penetrating when we see the similarities between their situation and our own.

In the first twelve verses, Paul is confronting the arguments by which his opponents in Thessalonica are maligning him. His response is not to ignore them, but to confute them. Firstly, by appealing to the Thessalonians' own experience of his ministry – 'You know, brothers...' (v. 1) and secondly, by clearly explaining to them why he did what he did. In verses 1-6, we have not so much a statement of the temptations to spurious ministry that we ought to avoid, but vigorous denial of what were scurrilous slanders being made against him. So I want to call verses 1-6a: *Refutation*, and verses 6b-12: *Affirmation*, because at that half-way point Paul piles up the metaphors to describe the positive motivation of his ministry. Then from verses 13-16, there is *Confirmation*, in terms of the Thessalonians response, which is expressed in renewed thanksgiving for the way they have received the gospel and are enduring, in spite of persecution.

1. Refutation (vv. 1-6a)

The opponents are clearly claiming, against all the evidence, of course, but nonetheless claiming it with great authority, that Paul's visit had been a failure (v. 1). The word means 'empty', 'hollow', 'useless'. Presumably they were saying that, because they had been successful in stirring up the riot in Thessalonica and getting Paul driven out of town. They were claiming that his failure to return proved that he had written off the Thessalonians and had no more real concern for them. Paul's response is to change the whole scenario (v. 2). He picks up the implicit criticisms of himself, and demonstrates that they cannot begin to stand up to analysis for a moment. His argument requires the Thessalonians to remember how he came to them from Philippi (v. 2). Far from being a profit-driven salesman, who sailed into Thessalonica to make a quick killing, having been driven away with his tail between his legs, Paul explains that it took nothing less than divine power to get him there at all. Verse 2 begins with a strong adversative, although it is not there in the NIV translation, but it actually begins with 'But...', 'on the contrary...', 'we had previously suffered and been insulted in Philippi, as you know.'

We know that in Philippi they were flogged and then put in the inner prison with their feet in the stocks – all quite illegal treatment for Roman citizens – no proper trial, no proper examination of the evidence, but it had happened (Acts 16:23-24). Undoubtedly, it left its own legacy of physical and emotional hurt in Paul and Silas. What Paul is saying in verse 2 is that it would have been the easiest thing in the world for him to conclude that he had misread the vision of the man from Macedonia saying, 'Come over and help us!' It would have been the easiest thing in the world to say, 'Well, it has been a long, hard haul, and I am long overdue for a break – what about that nice little academic job I saw advertised in the Hebrew University, surely that is what I am really being led to apply for?' It would have been the easiest thing in the world to turn his back on the gospel. To go on 'gospelling' in Thessalonica, and risk it all happening again, had required more than human courage. That is why he says it was with the help of our God (or literally, from the help of our God) that we even began to tell you the gospel. The very fact that he came at all was testimony to divinely-given strength, and once there, he didn't lie low but spoke out freely the gospel of God 'in spite of strong opposition', or more literally, 'amid great struggle'.

This introduces us to one of the characteristic words which Paul uses when he describes his ministry, the word *agon*. It is used in Philippians 1:30, at the end of that great chapter, where he talks about the Philippian church 'going through the same struggle you saw I had, and now hear that I still have'. The context there is persecution, where again they have to contend as one man for the gospel. Struggle is characteristic of apostolic ministry. In this case, it is external pressures, outward opposition (Phil. 1:30), going through the same struggle that Paul had and all of us will have if we are faithful to the gospel. Then in Colossians 2:1, he uses it internally: 'I want you to know how much I am struggling for you and for those at Laodicea, and for all who have not met me personally', and he goes on to show that he means struggling in prayer and labouring in this good work of interceding for their growth and their stability.

In picking up this metaphor from the athletic contests in the wrestling arena, Paul is graphically describing his authentic experience of gospel ministry, which always involves this sort of struggling. Moreover, in 1 Thessalonians 2:2, it is qualified by the description 'a great deal of', rendered in the NIV as 'strong' opposition. Why is this so important? Surely it is because it underlines the divine component without which ministry cannot happen. Paul would never have been there at all, doing this job, had it not been that the courage God gave him, the help of our God, enabled him to go forward in this gospel work. It is God's gospel, so the courage to speak it out is God's courage. No other power would have been great enough to overcome the apostle's natural human fear and hesitancy. So, if God's power is the secret behind the fact that he was there 'gospelling' at all, that must guarantee both the content of the message and the integrity of the messenger.

In verse 3, there are three specific focused denials – 'not error', 'not impurity', 'not deception'. 'For the appeal we make does not spring from error or impure motives, nor are we trying to trick you.' There is no doubt that while the apostolic messengers appealed to their hearers, a powerful persuasion was at work. Actually, the word translated 'appeal' is *paraklesis*, from the verb *parakaleo*, which is used of the Holy Spirit coming alongside to help, to strengthen, to exhort and to encourage. Of course, that sort of appeal was being made. Paul exhorted and encouraged them to believe. He did not preach the gospel in a 'take it or leave it' style. He desperately wanted his hearers to receive it and to believe it. But his motives were not those of the travelling religious conman. The message was not error, though the Jews refused to believe that Jesus is the Christ, and therefore branded Paul as a heretic. In verse 4, Paul will refute that on the grounds that it is God's gospel and it is God's call, so that it is God's infallible assessment that really matters.

'Not impurity.' The word is often used of sexual immorality, and it could be that Paul was being charged with that. Nothing is too low for the enemy when he is attacking gospel workers. But it may be used much more generally to indicate pride, greed, or any other mixed or false motive, which seems to be the more likely meaning. However hard they tried, these Jewish detractors could not make the mud of false motivation stick. Nor did he use deception. The Thessalonian believers were not tricked and deluded into their faith on the grounds of promises which he couldn't deliver. That was not why he came.

As refutation of these charges, Paul's strongest thread is his constant appeal to *God's* involvement in his ministry. 'The help of our God' (v. 2) is followed by 'we speak as men approved of God.... We are not trying to please men but God...' (v. 4). 'God is our witness' (v. 5). Interestingly, in verse 4, the same verb is used twice, translated in the NIV as 'approved', in the first occurrence, and then as 'tests' at the end of the verse. So what

Paul is claiming is that this God who called him to ministry and empowered him to do it, is the One who has approved him, and who goes on testing him. The verb is *dokimazo*, which means to test something so as to prove it, and then on the basis that it has passed the test, to approve it.

Perhaps we can illustrate the force of this verb from those television adverts for washing powder. They haven't varied much in thirty years or so! There is the poor harassed mother, looking absolutely at the end of her tether, in the kitchen, and in comes the son with all his soccer kit to wash, and everybody's kit from the whole team, and she says, 'How am I going to shift all this mud and grease and grass out of it?' So, she puts it through with her inferior washing powder (brand X) and it doesn't work because you can still see all the stains. But then the lady from next door comes in. She is twenty years younger, not a hair out of place, and seems to have all the time in the world to go around advising people on washing powder, and she says, 'What you want to use is Whizzo, and then you will have no more problems with the soccer kit.' One wash with Whizzo, and she takes out the clothes, holds them up to the light, and you see there is no stain anywhere on any of the kit. It is whiter than white. That's *dokimatzo*. You prove it, and then you approve it because it has been proved.

Now that is what is happening between God and Paul. 'He is proving me all the time,' Paul says. 'He has approved me in what I have done in the past – "we speak as men approved by God to be entrusted with the gospel." He called me, he arrested me on the road to Damascus, he commissioned me to be his apostle to the Gentiles, but he is the God who goes on testing me.' That is what ministry is about. All the time, God is testing our hearts. So the standard of reference would mean that Paul is not in the least wanting to deceive people, because although a preacher might skilfully pull the wool over human eyes, nothing can be hidden from God, and God's is the only assessment that ultimately matters. Paul is living his life out before God and wanting his approval, because it is God who has called him to be the apostle to the Gentiles. How then can his opponents turn round and claim that his motives are unworthy and that what he is doing is for his own ends? 'We are not trying to please men, but God who tests our hearts.'

Paul is very much aware that he is in the school of continuous assessment, and that this is not just in the external areas of his visible ministry, but in his innermost heart. That is what matters, for the vindication and effectiveness of his mission. To quote again F. F. Bruce: 'Only if they conducted themselves in a manner worthy of the gospel which they proclaimed, could they reasonably expect their converts to live in a manner worthy of the gospel which they received.'[2]

That is why he can go on, in verse 5, to say there has been neither flattery nor greed; no impure motives. And then he appeals to the facts of their experience of him while he was with them. Isn't that an amazing thing to be able to say? Of course, the world is not as näive about these things as we in the churches often are. Because we want to believe the best about others, Christians can sometimes be sitting ducks for unscrupulous religious salesmen. We cannot quite believe that someone coming in the name of Christ could actually be motivated by greed and self-interest, which is why so many are deluded and led astray. We are all susceptible to flattery, which is telling people what they want to hear about themselves, so that they will do what the flatterer wants them to do. And that will usually be to contribute to their kudos, by becoming a devoted follower, and to their friends, by becoming a sacrificial giver. This is the approach which plays on the emotions of defenceless people, which doesn't tell you the small print until you are committed, and then dictates what you are to do with your money, your time, your resources, and your very life. But that sort of religious 'ministry', so-called, is simply dedicated to building its own empire, to fleecing the gullible and to inflating personal glory and kudos. The cable and satellite channels are ready to pipe it into our homes. Send in your pledges in hard cash and we will send you a vial of healing water; we will pray for your sick relative; you will receive financial blessings unlimited – so long as you send it in *now* and so long as you send it to *us*.

The motivation for this distortion of Christian ministry is not too difficult to track. People want to have power and wealth, to be successful and applauded, so to acquire these things for yourself, while appearing to offer them to others, can seem to be an ideal combination. If you want to receive praise from men, that will be the obvious route to go. But that, Paul protests, is the very antithesis of real gospel ministry (v. 6). Paul's opponents may want to tar him with that brush, but all it will achieve is to highlight the contrast between religion as business and the gospel of Christ. Verse 6a is a marvellously liberating sentence: 'We were not looking for praise from men, not from you, or anyone else.' Now when you and I can say that, then we are free gospel servants. If our Christian service is motivated by wanting others to affirm us, to be pleased with us and to praise us, that will be all we have to hold on to when the going gets tough, but of course it won't be serving Christ at all. What we are actually doing when we fall into that temptation is to go back to the old idol shrine that is really dedicated to ourselves. The only corrective is to realise that, in the final analysis, human approval does not matter. If we fear men, so that deep down we are really looking for their approval, then we shall not fear God. But if we fear God, then we shall not fear men. And we all know how Christian ministry is so easily captivated by men, whether it is men within the local church, or whether it is denominational structures being operated by men; we all come under that sort of pressure. To be liberated from the desire for approval by others sets us free to start pleasing God.

Paul did not play to the gallery; he did not live for the crowd. That is why he would never compromise the message, his motives or his methods. One of his favourite Thessalonian words is 'blameless', and that is really at the heart of these first six verses. You may range all these charges against us, but can you prove them for one moment? No. We are blameless.

2. *Affirmation* (verses 6b-12)

This section is dominated by two pervasive comparisons, or models, of the relationship that Paul and Silas had with these new believers in Thessalonica. Verses 6b-9 concentrate on the picture of a mother caring for her baby, and verses 10-12 on the picture of a father instructing and exemplifying to his growing children the right way of living. Clearly this is a key paragraph for our understanding of apostolic ministry, and what it might mean for us to stand in that succession.

Verse 6b seems to include Silas and Timothy in the title 'apostle', which may indicate that Paul is using the term in its more general sense of 'missionary' rather than the narrower usage of divinely-commissioned witnesses of the risen Lord. What then did this ministry involve as one 'sent' by Christ? By way of answer, the paragraph concentrates on the specific task of communicating the gospel through relationships. At the heart of it, Paul declares, 'we were delighted to share with you not only the gospel of God but our lives as well' (v. 8). In fact, the structure of the paragraph leads us very clearly to that as the central idea.

There is a pattern, within the paragraph, of balancing ingredients, which leads us to its core, rather like a system of concentric circles. It can be represented in this way:

A – As apostles of Christ we could have been a burden
  B – We were gentle among you like a mother caring ...
    C – We loved you so much
      D – We were delighted to share with you not only the
             Gospel of God but our lives as well
    C^1 – You had become so dear to us
  B^1 – You remember, brothers, our toil and hardship
A^1 – In order not to be a burden to anyone while we preached
  the gospel

The balancing statements in both halves of the paragraph direct our attention to the heart of the matter in the middle (statement D). Here is the mark of authentic apostleship.

Messengers of Jesus share not only the gospel, but their own lives as well. They are not hired advertising agents, but personal representatives of the King of kings. Because their motivation is love, they are not a burden. Their focus, like a nursing mother, is always care for their children, whom they have brought to the birth in God's family. There is a bond of family love which transcends any formal or contractural relationships. They work hard, as every loving father does, to achieve the best for their children.

All this shows us that the apostolic preaching ministry is essentially one of self-giving and sharing one's life for the benefit of others. Of course, Paul's refutation of his accusers is still uppermost in his mind, so he calls on the positive evidence of his lifestyle – to support his previous denials (v. 9). There is no doubt in his mind about the right of the preacher to be supported by his hearers. He is going to elaborate that classically at a later date in 1 Corinthians 9, and it was obviously a feature of the first century church. But because that would have been a burden on the Thessalonians, Paul and Silas were prepared to work night and day – he describes it as 'toil and hardship'. And the phrase is almost exactly repeated in 2 Thessalonians 3:8, where he is using it to motivate the idle and rebuke them for their failure to work. He says, 'nor did we eat anyone's food without paying for it. On the contrary, we worked night and day, labouring and toiling so that we would not be a burden to any of you.'

This is quoted by Paul as proof of the genuineness of their relationship and evidence of the love that he has for them. Findlay paraphrases 2:6 as 'we might have sat heavily upon you'.[3] Obviously, the reference is primarily financial, but the use of the word 'gentle' in verse 7 is in direct contrast with the exploitation that he has just denied – gentleness is the opposite of being a heavy weight. It is an appropriate description of a nursing mother, and that in turn is a metaphor which very aptly describes this apostolic ministry, which has brought Paul's readers to the spiritual birth. They are his children in the faith and he cherishes them as a mother does her own babies.

The word for 'mother' is used for any woman who is breast-feeding a baby, and some of the older translations have 'nurse'. But the Greek says 'her own children', so the bond of personal relationship is what lies at the heart of Paul's imagery. The nursing mother shares her life with the child, which provides a beautiful picture of gospel work. If the nursing mother is feeding the child on demand, her whole life revolves around the child and its needs. No one would make that sort of sacrifice without maternal love being the motivator, and that is Paul's motive, expressed in very strong terms in verse 8: 'We loved you so much ... you had become so dear to us.'

Only God can produce a love like that, which is precisely why Paul appeals to it as a hallmark of true gospel ministry. It is interesting, too, that the tense of 'we were delighted' is the imperfect, that is, 'we kept on being delighted'. That's very challenging, isn't it? Yet this was the apostles' consistent attitude in Thessalonica. How can we share the gospel? How can we share ourselves? The temptation in Christian ministry today is to be delighted to share the gospel, particularly if it is a good congregation and everything seems to be going well, because you can share the gospel like that without any very great personal cost. But to share your life with people is a matter of self-denial, which is costly and demanding. Paul says that is what authenticated the message in Thessalonica.

Every Jewish rabbi had his trade, of course, but in the Greek world manual labour was generally despised and travelling teachers were graded in terms of their prestige by how good a living they made out of it. So, if you were actually working away, night and day, tent-making, what you were saying to the Greek world was that your message and methods were inferior because you could not actually make a living out of it. But you see, what Paul is concerned about is his motivation before God. His attitude was, 'I don't want to be a burden. I want to be like a gentle mother who nourishes you, and whatever the world may think about that doesn't really bother me, because I am not looking for praise from men, not from you or anyone else. I want my motivation to be right before God. He is the one who tests our hearts and he knows we are working night and day, because of our love for you.'

But of course the world will often get the motivation wrong, and make the wrong judgments. And a worldly church will judge by worldly standards. I remember a West African pastor telling me that his congregation had required his resignation because he was too poorly dressed. They had been deluded by the prosperity gospel teaching before he joined them, and so they were convinced that if he was a real man of God, the Lord would have prospered him. He would have dressed better, driven a better car and lived at a higher standard than the rest of the congregation. They wanted that sort of 'holy' man as their pastor, although I know that he literally laboured night and day in care for them. But they were not going to contribute to his support – that had to be miraculous by pennies (or pounds) from heaven.

The world will always make the wrong judgments, which is why we have got to be pleasing God and not pleasing men. But we do need to take the challenge on the chin, for ourselves too, in our Christian service. Of course, it is possible to work so hard and so unremittingly that we seize up, and yet it is equally possible, to potter, and to indulge our own interests, all with a view to sharing the gospel more effectively of course, but to be far less enthusiastic about sharing our lives. When the correctness of what we say becomes more important than the nurture of those who hear us, they are not as dear to us as they ought to be.

How can we proclaim a gospel of love authentically if our methods of evangelism are more like hit-and-run raids? There is nothing of the impersonal soap-box on the street corner here. There is nothing of the tract through the door and beetle down the path. I was in a church not long ago when they were actually exhorted to come and do this tract through the door business and the line to sell it was – 'You won't have to knock the doors or speak to anyone!' What does that say about us and our message? Spreading the gospel is not spraying large numbers at arms' length with a diluted solution of the message, like insect-

icide on roses. New Testament evangelism is loving friendship
that shares the life as well as the message. That is the cost, but it
is also the joy. We need to return to that perspective in our
technology-centred, methodology-obsessed generation. I am all
for encouraging people to know the joys of sharing the gospel
and having some sort of evangelistic methodology, but the
problem is that it always focuses on the end point, and everybody
judges it by whether or not we got to the end point. What this
passage says is that true 'gospelling' means that you cannot give
the message without giving the messenger. If we want to be
remote from people, we have chosen the wrong religion. Christ's
servants wash people's feet; they are devoted to fellowship. It is
about sharing our lives as a way of introducing our Lord, and
both our speech and our actions are vital.

It is not difficult, is it, to specialise in one or the other,
according to our temperament? But when you have both, there
you see the love of God in action. We must never forget that the
gospel of God introduces people to Christ. One of our current
dangers is that we just invite them to church, because for many
people that is what evangelism is – increased church attendance.
A gentleman informed me the other day that he was an
evangelical, liberal catholic. So I said to him, 'Would you mind
explaining to me what the evangelical bit in that means?' And
he said that it meant that he was positively in favour of church
growth. That is what people think evangelism is – numbers going
up; whereas, clearly here, it is sharing our lives with people to
such an extent that the very love and truth of God are incarnated
through the messenger and the reality of that gospel. That is
what produces a flagship church like Thessalonica. So, when
the enemies of the gospel come along and throw muck at the
messenger, a church like this pays no attention to them at all,
because its members know that they have experienced the reality
of true apostolic work.

The second picture reminds us that evangelism leads to
nurture. We move from the nursing mother to the father of the
growing child in the one long sentence which is verses 10-12.

Already Paul has called both God and the Thessalonians to witness to the truth of his defence and now he does so even more emphatically, joining the two of them together. Indeed, verses 10-12 are really a reinforced summary of verses 1-9. So verse 10a echoes verse 5 – 'You are witnesses and so is God.' Verse 10b summarises the content of verses 3, 4 and 6. Those false motives that he has left behind are now replaced with the true motives and the true evidence of 'how holy, righteous and blameless we were among you'. If then we have turned our backs on all those things, in order that we might be like a real mother caring for her children, think back and see how we lived also as a father working for the good of his family.

The little child, or baby, of verse 7, has now become the growing child of verse 11, and so the metaphor changes from the nursing mother to the increasing responsibility of the father. His responsibility is to encourage (v. 12) – that is *parakaleo*, again, the verb used for 'appeal' in verse 3. He must come alongside to help, to model the response that he is looking for. He must comfort, that is, he must put strength into his children, and urge them (the strongest of the three verbs), charge them, command them. It provides a good test for those of us who are fathers, doesn't it? Are we encouraging, comforting, urging our children? It is also a good test for us in ministry. Is this what we are doing in our churches? It is necessary to be devoted to developing lives which are 'worthy of God'. The literal meaning, 'to walk worthy of God', emphasizes a continuous progression of life which glorifies God by becoming increasingly like him.

Holy, righteous and blameless lives reflect the glory of the God who calls us in the gospel, and they bring him glory by demonstrating how his power at work in the individual can transform lives. The work of the father is to be a model to his children in this, to get alongside them to strengthen and to challenge them, to be someone who is worthy of the God 'who calls you into his kingdom and glory' (v. 12). Fascinatingly, the word translated 'glory' is the same word as 'praise' in verse 6. In this way, the theme is repeated. If I know that it is God's kingdom of glory I am being called into, then I will not be so worried about the praise of men. It is the eternal kingdom of the glory of God that I am being called to, and therefore I want to live a life worthy of him, says Paul, and I want you to do the same. We are all in this together and my role is to deal with you as a father with his children, to build you up so that the goal becomes a reality.

3. *Confirmation* (verses 13-16)

Just as Paul's consistent behaviour confirmed his message, so the behaviour of the Thessalonians is a confirmation that they have rightly received this true message, and that Paul's visit was indeed a manifestation of the power of God. Remember the big picture of what Paul is aiming to achieve. He wants to assure them that they are on track. They are a flagship church, but they must keep going in that direction. All of this is designed to undergird their faith, to strengthen their love, to show how that love labours, so that they themselves keep moving forward in these key areas. Several key words from chapter 1 are repeated here: the word of God, imitators, affliction, suffering. There is also a parallel movement in the thought content, moving from the entrance of the gospel, to the way it was received, and to the way it was implemented.

That is what Paul is writing about at the start of verse 13: 'And we also thank God continually because, when you received the word of God, which you heard from us, you accepted it not as the word of men, but as it actually is, the word of God, which is at work in you who believe.' This is similar to his emphasis in 1:5: 'our gospel came to you not simply with words, but also with power, with the Holy Spirit and with deep conviction.' Verse 13 is a commentary on that event. They received the gospel, gladly, joyfully, believingly, as the word of God, and that word is at work in them. But we have already been taught that faith without works is dead, that real faith produces work (1:3), so Paul now shows us that faith working out in practice. We know you have the real faith because the word is at work in you, and the word of God is producing a transformation in your lives. No merely human words can achieve that, but the word of God, revealing the will of God, is the only agency that can bring about such change. The proof that it is God's power is that you have become imitators of Christ, and you are imitating your fellow-Christians even though that means that you suffer from your own countrymen the same things the churches in Judea suffer from the Jews (v. 14).

That must have been a very important encouragement to the Thessalonian church. The suffering they are going through is not unusual, it is not unexpected, indeed it seems to be the norm for the church. So the Judean churches suffered from the Jews, their fellow countrymen, and now the Thessalonians are suffering from their fellow Greeks, and Paul is saying that is a mark of reality, which shows you are on track.

The last two verses are among the strongest words of accusation in the whole of the New Testament, which some readers of this letter have found very hard to take. How is it that after these statements about being a loving mother and a caring father, Paul can suddenly turn on his own people, the Jews, and use such violent language? They 'killed the Lord Jesus and the prophets and also drove us out'. Instead of using the normal word 'crucified', he uses the most violent verb he can find – who 'murdered' the Lord. It is as stark as it could be, but he is pointing out that this was no isolated crime, it was the climax of a long process. For those Jews who killed the Lord Jesus were of the same nation, the same community of people, who killed the prophets, and who now (the jealous Jews in Thessalonica) have driven out the messengers of Christ. He is aware that the opposition is coming from the Jews in the synagogue. They are the real opponents in Thessalonica, who are trying to destroy Paul as a gospel messenger, and to pull down what he has done. So he warns the Christians that if they are going to listen to the Jews, they should remember what the Jews have done. Remember that they killed the Lord Jesus, remember that they killed the prophets, and remember that they have driven out Paul and his companions, which is not surprising because 'they displease God and are hostile to all men in their effort to keep us from speaking to the Gentiles'. That is what is at the heart of it all: they don't want the Gentiles to hear the gospel. They want the Gentiles to become Jews. It's all about their jealousy, so when Paul comes in and removes all their Gentile converts from the Thessalonian synagogue, how are they going to react? There's only one possible answer. They are going to do everything they can to stop this man preaching to the Gentiles so that they may be saved. For the Jews, the only way the Gentiles can be reached is if they become members of their community by becoming God-fearers, and perhaps eventually being circumcised. There is no other way to go.

Now look at how Paul deals with this. 'Don't listen to that sort of criticism; look at my record in comparison. Look at how I lived among you, look at what the gospel has done in your lives, look at how gladly you received it, and how it is changing you, and don't listen to these lies because, sadly, they are part of a long record of opposition to the work of God. They displease God and are hostile to all men.' That is actually expressed in the original as two exclamations – 'How displeasing to God!' 'How hostile to everybody!' So, what they are attempting to do is to prevent the message of God's rescue from reaching the Gentiles (v. 16a) so that they may be saved.

Paul sees this entrenched opposition to the apostolic mission as the completion of the full total of those sins that have always been present in their rejection of God's words in the prophets and ultimately in his Son. The language is very daunting indeed. 'In this way they always heap up their sins to the limit.' In their opposition to the gospel going out to the Gentiles, we see the sum total of their rejection of Yahweh as the universal redeemer. And because we see sins to the limit, in this rejection of Christ, Paul says that the wrath of God will also be seen 'to the limit'. 'The wrath of God has come upon them at last,' or 'fully' as the NIV footnote puts it. They heap up their sins to the limit, but to reject God as redeemer, whether you are Jew or Gentile, is ultimately to experience the wrath of God, to the limit. The full weight of God's wrath is coming, as 1:10 reminds us, from which only Jesus can rescue us.

So the section ends on that eschatological note. These are issues of time and eternity, and the endurance of suffering like this is only possible because we know that God has called us to his kingdom of eternal glory. But equally, it is true that for those who reject Jesus, nothing remains but the coming wrath.

How powerfully re-affirming these marks of reality must have been to Paul's Thessalonian readers. They are a true group of believers; they have found the real God through Jesus, or rather he has found them and brought them into a true relationship with him. They have received an authentic gospel ministry. It was the word of God to them, proved by his power, that gave Paul courage to do the work and enabled him to reject all other motivations than that of pleasing the Lord. They had been on the receiving end of true gospel love, like a mother caring for a little child, like a father encouraging his growing children. All of that is proof of reality, and when they look at themselves they can see further proof, because this word which was proclaimed to them has been received, not just as human words, but as the word of God. So don't listen to the detractors, don't turn your back on this gospel, don't allow the tempter to entice you away from this truth. See it all in the light of eternity. The wrath of God is coming; the only way of rescue is through Jesus, his Son from heaven. You have turned and are serving, as you wait for him. So keep on track, because you have believed the real gospel message and are experiencing the true gospel relationships.

4

A Love that Labours (2)
1 Thessalonians 2:17-3:13

[17]But, brothers, when we were torn away from you for a short time (in person, not in thought), out of our intense longing we made every effort to see you. [18]For we wanted to come to you – certainly I, Paul, did, again and again – but Satan stopped us. [19]For what is our hope, our joy, or the crown in which we will glory in the presence of our Lord Jesus Christ when he comes? Is it not you? [20]Indeed, you are our glory and joy.

[1]So when we could stand it no longer, we thought it best to be left by ourselves in Athens. [2]We sent Timothy, who is our brother and God's fellow-worker in spreading the gospel of Christ, to strengthen and encourage you in your faith, [3]so that no-one would be unsettled by these trials. You know quite well that we were destined for them. [4]In fact, when we were with you, we kept telling you that we would be persecuted. And it turned out that way, as you well know. [5]For this reason, when I could stand it no longer, I sent to find out about your faith. I was afraid that in some way the tempter might have tempted you and our efforts might have been useless.

[6]But Timothy has just now come to us from you and has brought good news about your faith and love. He has told us that you always have pleasant memories of us and that you long to see us, just as we also long to see you. [7]Therefore, brothers, in all our distress and persecution we were encouraged about you because of your faith. [8]For now we really live, since you are standing firm in the Lord. [9]How can we thank God enough for you in return for all the joy we have in the presence of our God because of you? [10]Night and day we pray most earnestly that we may see you again and supply what is lacking in your faith.

[11]Now may our God and Father himself and our Lord Jesus clear the way for us to come to you. [12]May the Lord make your love increase and overflow for each other and for everyone else, just as ours does for you. [13]May he strengthen your hearts so that you will be blameless and holy in the presence of our God and Father when our Lord Jesus comes with all his holy ones (1 Thess. 2:17–3:13).

We come now to what is the most personal section of the letter, and I want to try to enter into Paul's heart here, because it seems to me this section is the heart-beat of the letter as he uncovers for us his own particular concerns. It is not just that Paul opens his heart to them and so to us, but that we see the perspective of his relationship with his converts, which governed his entire ministry and which becomes such a central theme for this letter as a whole. Look at it this way. As Paul looks to the future, in the midst of all his present suffering and distress, what is it that most warms and rejoices his heart? 'What is our hope, our joy, or the crown in which we will glory in the presence of our Lord Jesus Christ when he comes? Is it not you? Indeed, you are our glory and joy' (2:19). That is a remarkable thing to say, that when he looks to the future what he is going to rejoice in on the day of Christ is the Thessalonian believers.

Similarly, if he reflects on his present situation, where does he find his joy and encouragement? 'How can we thank God enough for you in return for all the joy we have in the presence of our God because of you?' (3:9) That is equally striking. This is no mere professional relationship, like a doctor with a patient, or a counsellor with a client. There is a depth of personal commitment and friendship between Paul and his converts, which will last for eternity. In that sense, it provides a profound challenge to our business models of ministry, which often pervade contemporary conferences and training courses. While we want to be business-like, we are not running the church as a business, although we can almost imperceptibly adopt those norms in assessing ourselves and our work. Paul's task is very clearly defined, but his orientation is not just to the task; it is supremely to the people. It is a relational ministry, and this section makes that abundantly plain.

The apostle is still defending himself from the accusation that because he has made no return visit to Thessalonica, and has shown no sign of bothering with them, he has no real and lasting interest in them as people. He began that refutation with his summons to them to recall the motherly and fatherly care he demonstrated when he was with them, and implicitly asks the questions, 'Could that have been artificial or unreal? Would I have worked night and day if I didn't really care?' He would have had to be a very skilled dissembler, but you know how devastatingly let down young Christians can be when what they thought was genuine Christian love is not sustained. Paul is a realist, who knows that he has been away so long from Thessalonica, that it may well be some people are actually beginning to believe the lies that are being told about him. Those of us who have had any dealings with teenagers know how important that sort of genuine Christian love is for tender, growing plants. What about the camp or mission leader, who seems to take a special interest in a young person while the camp is on, but never writes or phones afterwards, and who, at the reunion, is far more interested in their peer-group of leaders than the children? You hear this sort of thing happening so often because such ministry is task-oriented, rather than people-oriented. But real gospel work is always relational.

Just recently, I spoke to a keen, young Christian, who had been specially befriended and discipled by his small group leader, so successfully that he himself was selected for leadership of a similar group, in that church, the next year. However, when he went to the leaders' training evening, he was really rather frightened to discover that all the 'spontaneous' fellowship he thought he had enjoyed, had actually been planned and scripted, and now he was expected to model exactly the same techniques with other people. A methodology like that could be the vehicle of genuine Christian love, but relationships that are switched on or off, according to the degree of conformity to the norms of the sub-culture, are surely pseudo-relationships, which are profoundly sub-Christian, and often positively damaging.

There is, of course, a major qualitative difference between the Thessalonian context and our own. It is very difficult for us to start completely from scratch, as Paul did. Even if we plant new churches, we usually do so with a nucleus of fellow-Christians, who all have a background which they bring with them. Most of us belong to congregations which have existed for some time, often several generations, and have all sorts of inherited traditions. We all know how existing church members look back to previous ministries, through which they came to faith, usually through very rose-tinted spectacles – those were the golden days – and how their affection and loyalty always gravitate back to their spiritual father. That seems to me to be entirely natural, even inescapable. I don't think we can possibly work in any other context. So while we are all committed, as fellow-workers in the gospel, to the *agape* that seeks the very best for all our church members, we shouldn't be surprised that some of them are inevitably closer to us than others. What I think we can learn from Paul in his relationship with this church is that his Christian service is bound up with the people for whom he is responsible before God. His authenticity as a minister of Christ and of the gospel is seen in his willingness to spend and be spent for others, to encourage their growth in faith and love, holiness and hope.

There is nothing at arms-length about Paul's ministry. Even though he is physically separated from them by many miles, he is utterly committed to them, and all his writing and praying is for one purpose, that the flock will be nurtured. Unless that is very clearly the motivation, it is possible to be drawn to the full-time ministry for the wrong reasons. Some of us have a natural delight and propensity for study and we can be tempted to embrace the ordained ministry in order to give ourselves to the study of the Word and prayer, which are obviously clear biblical priorities. But if our study becomes something of a refuge from the congregation, then we have got it wrong. Some of us may be more gifted administratively than others, but if the church office becomes my refuge from the church, again it is wrong. If the gospel combines objective truth and relational love, so must its ministers. Paul is no 'ivory tower' theorist. It is a true shepherd-heart that galvanises him into action, for the benefit of the Thessalonian church, so that he may fulfil his calling and they may fulfil their potential. But that sort of service implies vulnerability, which is the dominating theme of these verses.

We shall divide the section into four paragraphs, starting with 2:17-20, where Paul is explaining why he has not been able to return to Thessalonica.

> '17But, brothers, when we were torn away from you for a short time (in person, not in thought), out of our intense longing we made every effort to see you. 18For we wanted to come to you – certainly I, Paul, did, again and again – but Satan stopped us. 19For what is our hope, our joy, or the crown in which we will glory in the presence of our Lord Jesus Christ when he comes? Is it not you? 20Indeed, you are our glory and joy.'

The use of 'brothers' here, at the start of the section, is not empty. It is further evidence of the relationship which the gospel has brought them into. The family tone has already been strong, with the mother/father imagery; now it is the same sort of family relationship but in terms of brothers. When they had to escape from Thessalonica to Berea, Paul and Silas felt, he says, like parents bereaved of their children. That is implied in the verb 'torn away' from you. It is a verb that usually means 'orphaned'. This was a painful, unnatural severance, with all the shock and hurt that involves, although when it happened, Paul was hopeful that it would be for a short time – literally, for the space of an hour. He had hoped to be able to get back to them soon. But as he writes, it is still continuing, probably a year, or longer, after the event. What he wants to stress is that he has always been trying throughout that period to get back to them if he possibly could. To suggest that he fled with a huge sigh of relief and put an end to his interest in Thessalonica is a monstrous accusation. On the contrary, they were never out of his thoughts, and the evidence is to be seen in the strenuous efforts he has made to revisit them. The language is very strong: 'we stirred ourselves excessively, with great desire, to come to you.'

Verses 19-20 show that the motivation was deeper than a desire on Paul's part to finish off the job, as it were. The future hope connected to the return of Christ has powerful effects on the present faith and love of the apostle. Again, the language is broken, the emotion is clearly very intense. The reason why the Thessalonians are so precious to him is not only because of his time with them there and because of his life involvement with them, but ultimately the reason is an eternal one. They are his hope, his joy and his crown of exaltation. The picture is of the athlete's laurel wreath, the gold medal, at the end of the race. When Paul gets to the end and receives the reward, what will it be? He says that the Thessalonian Christians will be his hope, his joy and his crown. So it is on their faithfulness and perseverance that Paul's confidence of reward for his faithful service depends.

This dominating concern of Paul for his eternal reward is not without its problems. Some commentators, very concerned about this 'crown of glory' (or literally, 'crown of pride'), are reluctant to attribute any motives of self-interest to the apostle. But surely this is to indulge a false humility and a pseudo-spirituality. We know that Paul sees the whole gospel enterprise as entirely an initiative of God's grace, which includes his own calling to be the apostle to the Gentiles. He has told us already that it is all of God. But he knows that while his salvation is secure, his work will be judged, to determine the reward that he will receive. So he wants it to be found to be enduring, he wants it to be of quality, and he wants the judgment and assessment at the last day to be one of hope, joy and glory.

If that is embarrassing to us, perhaps we have not yet got a taste of New Testament realism. Surely it is this same perspective which we ought to have? We are travelling to the same destination. The time-line leads inevitably to the day of the Lord's appearing when we shall all stand before the judgment seat of Christ. As our service is assessed, on that great day, will it not be a great joy, a fulfilment of hope and the ultimate crown of glory if, in the grace and mercy of God, those with whose lives we have been involved in our work on earth are there with us in the Lord's presence? That perspective casts a very different light on our present priorities.

This leads us to the second problem, which is that we do not have anything like the sense of the importance of the *parousia,* the coming of the Lord, that Paul has. At this point, he introduces this key word which he is going to use six times in the rest of the letter, while he only uses it once in the whole of the rest of his writings. The other time he uses it is 1 Corinthians 15:23, where, speaking about the resurrection he says, 'Christ, the first-fruits, then, at his parousia, those who belong to him.' The term is used in Matthew and elsewhere in the New Testament writings of James, Peter and John, but here is clearly the definitive usage in Paul, and the focus of the letter now begins to move in on the parousia, so that when we get to chapters 4 and 5, we see just how strong this theme is.

There can be little doubt that Paul's thinking about the parousia is very different from our own, 1900 years later. Perhaps part of the problem for us is that we tend to think about the coming of Jesus as the 'second' coming. We seem to lose something of the impact of the word *parousia*, because of this. Originally, the term was used of a royal visit to a city, which would include all the appropriate ceremonies and honours. If the Roman emperor was going to come to your city, then he would be met at a distance by a delegation before he arrived, who would bestow honours upon him, and give to him the most lavish gifts that the city could afford. This would be reciprocated as the emperor honoured the city and rewarded its loyal citizens. A royal visit would be a day to remember. But, the first coming of Jesus wasn't like that at all! The first coming was to a life of humiliation and suffering, culminating in the cross. His glory was veiled; he died in shame and ignominy. The only event that can make full sense of that coming is the parousia. Then Jesus will be revealed as the Lord of Glory, and it will be a coming utterly different from the incarnation. Then he will be recognized as the divine Sovereign, who brings salvation to his people, but judgment and condemnation to his enemies, on the day when all will honour him and he will honour his faithful servants. That stands in the direct line from the Old Testament 'day of the

Lord', when God visits his people to judge and to reward them. In the same event he moves in both salvation and judgment. Indeed, 1:10 has told us that salvation is the visitation of his judgment.

For Paul, then, the parousia is not just the end point of history, which is the way we often think about it. For Paul, it is the climax and fulfilment of the ages. It is *the* event which makes sense of the present suffering. It is *the* great motivator to keep pressing on, even though one's current experience is persecution and oppression. That is why we have that telling little phrase at the end of verse 18: 'Satan stopped us.' Our present experience in gospel work today is that Satan can and does hinder. It is idle to speculate in what specific way that happened, but it would be more foolish to ignore its reality as a dimension of gospel work. Certainly, Paul is not rushing to this as an excuse for human failure, which is why he says he made every effort repeatedly to get back to see them. He is not like the preacher who cannot be bothered to prepare and says, 'The devil stopped me from getting to work this week.' By contrast, Paul made every effort, out of intense longing, all the time trying to get back to see them. But it is a reality that gospel work can be hindered by Satan. We know, of course, that the devil can only act within the permissive will of God, and the book of Job in its opening chapter is the classic text for that truth. However, this was part of God's overruling providence, and surely Paul was right to see it also as Satanic activity fighting against the gospel. He makes the same point in 3:5, when he says, 'I was afraid that in some way the tempter might have tempted you and our efforts might have been useless.'

It is also instructive to see that Paul does not claim to have a personal authority, or to take authority, against Satan. The context leaves us in no doubt that if he could have done, he would have done. But the present experience of gospel ministry is not yet the sphere in which Christ's total victory over Satan is fully demonstrated. That awaits the parousia. The same point is made in 2 Thessalonians 2:8-10. Paul has been talking about 'the man of lawlessness', whom we will consider later. He writes:

'⁸And then the lawless one will be revealed, whom the Lord Jesus will overthrow with the breath of his mouth and destroy by the splendour of his coming. ⁹The coming of the lawless one will be in accordance with the work of Satan displayed in all kinds of counterfeit miracles, signs, and wonders, ¹⁰and in every sort of evil that deceives those who are perishing. They perish because they refused to love the truth and so be saved.'

It is a salutary reminder of just how active and powerful Satan is in this world. Through counterfeit miracles, signs and wonders, he produces every sort of evil to deceive people. He can only be stopped by a greater power, revealed in the coming of the Lord Jesus, when he will overthrow the lawless one. Until then, Satan is given a certain amount of power. So when Paul says, 'Satan hindered us', he is not finding some super-pious reason to excuse what had not happened. Opposition like that is a reality of gospel ministry. The parousia is so exciting because on that day every knee will bow, every tongue confess that Jesus Christ is Lord. Satan and all his agents will be forced to submit to the true authority of God, demonstrated in Christ's return. Until then, gospel ministry will include longing and anticipation, but the more clearly that far horizon dominates the present, the more faithful our service will be.

In the second section (3:1-5), Paul shows us some of his own fears and frustration.

'¹So when we could stand it no longer, we thought it best to be left by ourselves in Athens. ²We sent Timothy, who is our brother and God's fellow-worker in spreading the gospel of Christ, to strengthen and encourage you in your faith, ³so that no-one would be unsettled by these trials. You know quite well that we were destined for them. ⁴In fact, when we were with you, we kept telling you that we would be persecuted. And it turned out that way, as

you well know. ⁵For this reason, when I could stand it no longer, I
sent to find out about your faith. I was afraid that in some way the
tempter might have tempted you and our efforts might have been
useless.'

There is great honesty in this section, and great encouragement
too, as we realize that Paul's fears about the situation were very
much like our own. The awful possibility, yawning like a chasm
at his feet, as he waited for word from Timothy about what was
happening in Thessalonica, is captured in the last word of verse
5 – 'useless'. It is exactly the same word which is translated
'failure' in 2:1. This was what his detractors were claiming about
his visit, and his greatest fear was that it might yet prove to be
so.

His anxiety is expressed in two practical possibilities. He
feared that the trials they had suffered might have unsettled some
(3:3). Closely connected to this, he feared that such unsettled
people might have been tempted away from the gospel and
diverted from God's revealed truth, believing Satan's lies (3:5).
While Paul undoubtedly had tremendous confidence in God's
power to keep, it does seem as though he was really troubled by
the situation. Notice how he says at the beginning of verse 5: 'I
could stand it no longer', a repetition of the clause with which
the chapter began (3:1) meaning 'when we could hold out no
longer against the pressure'. Paul had to know what was
happening. How desperate it would be if this church, about which
every one seemed to be talking, had failed to live up to its
reputation and drifted away from the truth of the gospel.

The other thing which encourages Paul as he looks back on
his own ministry among them is that he had been realistic about
the cost. As they faced pressures and trials the Thessalonians
knew quite well that they were destined for them. When he had
been ministering the gospel to them and nurturing the new
Christians, it had been part of his agenda that they should be
prepared for the trials to happen. He hadn't been persuading
them by error or tricks to sign up for an unrealistic Christian life

in this world. Paul had prepared them for pressure and problems, and he also sent Timothy to extend that ministry by targeting their need. He came to strengthen and encourage them in their faith (3:2). Notice how important faith is all the way through. 'I sent to find out about your faith' (3:5), that is the key thing. If they are holding on, it is because of their faith in God and in the gospel and their refusal to be diverted by all the attacks that are made against him.

Our third section (3:6-10) is concerned with Paul's rejoicing and thanksgiving for the news that Timothy has now brought him.

> [6]But Timothy has just now come to us from you and has brought good news about your faith and love. He has told us that you always have pleasant memories of us and that you long to see us, just as we also long to see you. [7]Therefore, brothers, in all our distress and persecution we were encouraged about you because of your faith. [8]For now we really live, since you are standing firm in the Lord. [9]How can we thank God enough for you in return for all the joy we have in the presence of our God because of you? [10]Night and day we pray most earnestly that we may see you again and supply what is lacking in your faith.

This section fits very closely with the big-picture thinking in Thessalonians which we are beginning to see with greater clarity. The marks of reality, that Christians really are on track, are their works resulting from faith, their labouring in love and their enduring hope. These are the qualities Paul has demonstrated consistently in his own life and in his gospel ministry. Now Timothy returns with the splendid news that the Thessalonians are demonstrating the same qualities of genuine Christianity. They are still holding firm to their faith in Jesus to rescue them from the coming wrath, and they are still serving the living and true God. They are reciprocating towards Paul the same quality of love he has for them, and so Timothy can return with the good news that 'you always have pleasant memories of us and that you long to see us, just as we long to see you' (3:6). If we want to learn from the big-picture thinking of the letter, it clearly brings before us the qualities which we ought to be looking for in our churches. Do we demonstrate these marks of reality and assurance which convinced Paul of this infant church's authentic Christian discipleship? 'Therefore, brothers, in all our distress and persecution we were encouraged about you because of your faith' (v. 7). That relationship was obviously extremely important to him.

It is an interesting observation that Timothy's good news produces in Paul the same results the gospel had produced in the Thessalonians. In fact, he actually describes Timothy as having come and 'evangelised' about their faith and love. That is the verb – he brought 'good news'. Just as the good news of Christ brought life and joy to them, so Timothy's good news brought life and joy to Paul. 'For now we really live... How can we thank God... for all the joy we have in the presence of our God' (vv. 8-9). So where the gospel is at work, it produces new life which is a cause of enormous joy, and where the gospel is being sustained and there is good news about faith and love, then those who hear it find their life is enriched as a result.

The second half of verse 6 introduces a further dimension of Paul's delight in knowing that his relationship with them is intact, undamaged by the accusations of his enemies. This underscores how very important the personal relationships are. It is such a relief to know that those Jewish slanders have had no real impact on them. So, the longing for renewed fellowship is mutual and they are not holding his failure to revisit them against him in any way. Just as his greatest concern was for their faith, so now his greatest joy and encouragement is to know that their faith is strong.

But there is also a new and important note which is introduced in verses 9 and 10. After thanking God for all the joy and encouragement brought to him by the constancy of the Thessalonian Christians, Paul adds, 'Night and day we pray most earnestly that we may see you again and supply what is lacking in your faith.' And that little note provides a forward pointer to what is going to come in chapters 4 and 5. Although there is great and genuine joy over the fact that they are standing firm, Timothy's report has obviously also indicated some areas where they need some help. So, as Paul's joy turns to prayer, it is that he might be able to come to see them and help them further. Until that happens, a letter will have to do, but what Paul desires most of all is to 'supply what is lacking in your faith'. The word translated 'supply' is that vivid verb which is used of mending nets in Mark 1:19, or in Ephesians 4:12 about equipping the saints for the work of ministry. It is making good the deficiencies, or restoring something to its proper usefulness, mending the holes in the net so that the net can do the job and you can catch the fish. Timothy has told him that there are some holes in the net. Obviously, he had only been with them such a short time! There are aspects of their faith that ought to be sorted out, and he is going to teach them about that in the next chapter, so there is just that little forward touch there. Their faith is strong, their love is real, and that is the cause of great rejoicing, but there is more to be done and Paul is keen to do it, so he prays on.

In the last section (3:11-13), we are told what this earnest prayer 'night and day' is all about.

> [11]Now may our God and Father himself and our Lord Jesus clear the way for us to come to you. [12]May the Lord make your love increase and overflow for each other and for everyone else, just as ours does for you. [13]May he strengthen your hearts so that you will be blameless and holy in the presence of our God and Father when our Lord Jesus comes with all his holy ones.

There are here three great desires which Paul expresses in terms of intercession. In verse 11 his desire to visit them. 'May our God and Father himself and our Lord Jesus clear the way for us to come to you.' Satan has stopped us; Lord, please clear the way. In verse 12 his desire is for their love towards one another to increase and overflow, and he uses himself as a model there. And then, verse 13 expresses his concern that they will persevere until the parousia, that great climax of the ages. Clearly, these last two requests, for their love to be increasing and overflowing and for their hope to persevere, carry with them spiritual exhortation. He tells them this, not just simply so that they may have the information that he is praying about it, but so that knowing his heart for them, they will be constrained in the same direction for themselves. It could hardly be put more straight-forwardly than in the opening verse of chapter 4: 'Finally, brothers, we instructed you how to live in order to please God, as in fact you are living. Now we ask you and urge you in the Lord Jesus to do this more and more.' That is the great thrust of what is going to come. He is going to instruct them, in chapters 4 and 5, how to live to please the Lord Jesus more and more, which is what he is praying for, so that they will be blameless and holy when he comes.

Perhaps the most significant ingredient of all in the last few verses, however, is a theme which we have not really noticed yet, but which is there just beneath the surface throughout both letters. It is the relationship of 'our Lord Jesus' with God the Father, seen to be one of perfect unity and equality. As one of the earliest New Testament letters, Thessalonians teaches this central doctrine of the Christian faith in the most unassuming way. In fact, it runs all the way through both letters, but without any great point being made about it, or attention drawn to it, which makes its testimony all the more eloquent and impressive. Here are the earliest expressions of that foundational Christology which motivated Paul's life and ministry so powerfully and for so long.

Who Jesus is

From time to time, hostile scholarship insists that nowhere in Paul's writings can the unequivocal statement be found that Jesus is God. Various proof texts have been advanced, such as 1 Corinthians 8:6, with resulting arguments about the translation.

But both the Thessalonian letters everywhere assume the equality
of the Father and the Son within the Trinity. It is here in this
section, at the very heart of the letter. Both God the Father and
our Lord Jesus Christ are petitioned equally in verse 11. Even
more significantly, verse 12 addresses Jesus alone, for he is
certainly the *kyrios*, the Lord, who is being referred to as the
One who can make their love increase. Further in verse 13, to
appear before our God and Father is also to appear before our
Lord Jesus when he comes. So again the parousia vocabulary
picks up the Old Testament imagery of Yahweh revealing
himself in glory, attended by his heavenly host, and applies it to
the Lord Jesus. Yahweh, then, is Jesus; Jesus is Yahweh. Of
course, our understanding of Yahweh in the Old Testament must
be Trinitarian – not just God the Father, but God the Father,
God the Son and God the Holy Spirit, the three persons in one
Godhead. The fascinating thing in Thessalonians is its spontaneous attribution to the Son of co-equality in deity with the
Father, which is far more eloquent than any formal credal
statement would be, and this within twenty years of the
crucifixion.

This prayer, right at the centre of 1 Thessalonians, is matched
in 2 Thessalonians by an equally central prayer that comes in
2:16-17, making the same point with crystal clarity: 'May our
Lord Jesus Christ himself and God our Father, who loved us
and by his grace gave us eternal encouragement and good hope,
encourage your hearts and strengthen you in every good deed
and word.' The significant factor here is that not only are the
two – our Lord Jesus Christ and God the Father – clearly co-
equal, but the Lord Jesus is actually placed first. The point is
being made quite artlessly, that in Paul's theology the Father
and the Son are completely equal, just as Jesus himself declared,
'I and the Father are one' (John 10:30).

Although some would want to qualify this, claiming that he
is describing them as being equal in purpose and action, that
seems to be an unnecessary distinction. He is clearly talking
about them being one in essence. Again, both letters point out

some ways in which that becomes clear. 1 Thessalonians 2:12 speaks of 'encouraging... you to live lives worthy of God, who calls you into his kingdom and glory'. And what is his kingdom and glory? 2 Thessalonians 2:14 answers, 'He called you to this through our gospel, that you might share in the glory of our Lord Jesus Christ.' So the final glory is God's glory, and the final glory is Christ's glory. There is no sense of them being different.

Consider how the Lord Jesus is invoked as the one to whom all authority belongs. 1 Thessalonians 4:1 says, 'we ... urge you in the Lord Jesus', or in the very next verse, 'you know what instructions we gave you by the authority of the Lord Jesus.' It is equally clear in the second letter: 'In the name of the Lord Jesus Christ, we command you, brothers' (3:6); 'Such people we command and urge in the Lord Jesus Christ to settle down and earn the bread they eat' (3:12). That is really a reflection of the prayer in 2 Thessalonians 3:5: 'May the Lord direct your hearts into God's love and Christ's perseverance.' So the Lord Jesus is the one who directs his people's hearts. Paul is looking for Christ to do what no mere man could ever begin to do. None of the prayers to the Lord Jesus in these verses could possibly be answered in the slightest degree by a mere human being – and a dead one at that! The deity of Christ is implicit all the way through the letters. It is not a controversy, but an essential cornerstone of the faith. If you want primitive Christology, here it is! In the very first verse of 1 Thessalonians Paul writes, 'To the church of the Thessalonians in God the Father and the Lord Jesus Christ.' The relationship to Jesus as Lord and Christ defines the church. And again in 1 Thessalonians 1:3, many of the commentators point out that the three key phrases, faith that works, love that labours, hope that endures, are placed between two divine statements: 'We continually remember before our God and Father' ... 'in our Lord Jesus Christ.'

When you get to the end of the letter the same thing is happening. In 1 Thessalonians 5:18, Paul writes: 'Give thanks in all circumstances, for this is God's will for you in Christ Jesus.'

The will of God is summed up in Christ Jesus. He is the one in whom that will resides; the one who always did the things that pleased the Father. He is the one who is the perfect representation of the Father. The same note is there in the great prayer at the end: 'May God himself, the God of peace, sanctify you through and through. May your whole spirit, soul and body be kept blameless at the coming of our Lord Jesus Christ. The one who calls you is faithful and he will do it' (5:23). The faithful God of peace, who sanctifies the believer, does this in view of the coming of the Lord Jesus. It is when Jesus appears that the kingdom comes and the glory is revealed, so no wonder the good news is called the gospel of God (2:2, 8), the gospel of Christ (3:2), and the gospel of our Lord Jesus (2 Thess. 1:8).

We could go on multiplying the instances. Someone has calculated ninety-five uses of Jesus, Christ or Lord referring to Jesus in the two letters. But the fascinating thing to me is that Paul is nowhere discussing the person of Christ, or coming anywhere near to writing a Christological treatise. He is telling a keen, but still immature group of Christians, who are on track but have a long way to go, and who are living in a violently hostile world, what they most need to hear to encourage them to keep on keeping on. Above everything else, they need to keep their eyes fixed on Jesus, the coming King. In fact, the whole idea of the parousia is meaningless if he is not the Lord Jesus Christ. There is nothing docetic about Paul's view, no diminution of Christ's real humanity here, but all the time he ascribes to him the attributes of deity, not least the fact that he will bring in the day of the Lord, that he is coming with his holy ones, and that we shall need divine strength if we are to be blameless and holy in his presence. That is why he prays.

For that great event, like Paul, we need to be planning and we need to be praying too. The tasks God has given us today will find a much needed new perspective as we see them in the light of that great day, the climax of the ages when the King appears

in all his glory, when the Lord Jesus Christ comes with all his
holy ones. What will be *our* joy and delight in that day? Like
Paul, it will be other people. It will be those who, by God's
grace, have a share in the glory because we were prepared to be
vulnerable in our gospel ministry to them. That is the authentic
gospelling, which is keeping on track.

Taking Stock ...
The story so far

Now that we have reached the half-way mark in the first letter, we need to step back for a pause to look over the terrain we have been travelling and to reflect on what we have seen and learned. The more clearly we can see the shape of the wood, the more we shall appreciate the variety and purpose of the individual trees. So, what have we discovered thus far about the big picture of 1 Thessalonians, its purpose and themes?

The Thessalonian church had a great beginning. Chapter 1 tells us that their faith in God was very widely known so that the cause of the gospel in Greece and mainland Europe was firmly nailed to the mast of this flagship church. But the great start had been followed rapidly by strong pressures and attacks, which Paul describes in chapter 3 as 'trials and testings', and which he is very concerned might have unsettled them. He fears that 'in some way the tempter might have tempted you so that our efforts might have been useless' (3:5). He himself had been hounded out of Thessalonica before the young church could be really rooted and nurtured to his satisfaction and then the same thing had happened in Berea and at Athens, where while a few responded to the gospel, many sneered and despised him. Not surprisingly, he moved on to Corinth in 'weakness and fear', as he says in 1 Corinthians 2:3, 'and with much trembling'. And it is while he is at Corinth that he hears news of the church and then writes 1 Thessalonians.

Doubtless, part of that fear and trembling was his apprehension about what might happen to him in a pagan hot-spot like Corinth, but we know from this letter that he was also very concerned indeed about the Thessalonian church. This key

church, his flag-ship church, occupied his mind. Will they hold
on to the gospel or are they going to be diverted from it, in
which case all that he could look back on could be the emptiness
of his visit and the failure of his ministry. That was why he
came on from Athens alone, sending Timothy back to
Macedonia, and it is Timothy's return that prompts the letter.
'Timothy has just now come to us from you and has brought
good news about your faith and love. He has told us that you
always have pleasant memories of us and that you long to see
us, just as we also long to see you. Therefore, brothers, in all our
distress and persecution, we were encouraged about you because
of your faith. For now we really live, since you are standing
firm in the Lord.' As a result, this theme of rejoicing and
thanksgiving runs all the way through 1 Thessalonians.

Paul's fears were certainly not without justification. The trials
had been severe. The jealous Jews we read about in Acts 17 had
blackened Paul's name, asserting that he had, quite intentionally,
left the Thessalonians in the lurch. It just proved that he was
only another religious salesman. They also seem to have claimed
that the Gentile persecution to which he refers in 2:14 – 'You
suffered from your own countrymen, the same things those
churches in Judea suffered from the Jews' – was further evidence
of the false character of the message they had believed, and of
their stupidity in coming out from under the umbrella of Judaism
when they left the synagogue. But the Thessalonians had not
given way. The tempter had not beguiled them.

The first three chapters are therefore full of thanksgiving and
assurance. Paul is piling up the proof of the reality of their
spiritual experience, so that they will continue to stand firm. He
confirms that they have believed God's authentic message,
presented faithfully to them by God's authentic messenger, since
both message and messenger are under scrutiny. The proof lies
not only in the objective realities of what God has done in time
and space in history. This is the gospel in which they have put
their faith and includes the hope that they have of the coming of
the Lord. These are great objective truths on which the church

is founded, but also – and this is the distinctive thing – the proof of reality is in their experience of that truth, working out in their lifestyle. Faith works, love labours, hope perseveres (1:3). It is not just that they believe right, but that their right believing leads to right living, and what they saw in the lives of their missionaries is now being demonstrated in their own lives too. They continue to welcome the message with joy (1:6), to believe it and to relay it to others. All this is in spite of severe suffering. God must be at work for this to happen. It is also the mark of the *word* of God at work. 'We also thank God continually because, when you received the word of God, which you heard from us, you accepted it not as the word of men, but as it actually is, the word of God, which is at work in you who believe' (2:13). These assurances which Paul gives are marks we should expect to see still in the church where the word of God is truly at work.

This is where Thessalonica begins to impact our contemporary culture. Here are the benchmarks by which we can still distinguish the genuine from the spurious. Since the Thessalonian Christians really are standing firm in the Lord, all those marks of reality, which are discovered in message and life, are tests which need to be applied to any and every claim to a work of the Lord in our generation.

But Timothy's visit has also revealed some holes in the net. There are deficiencies which need to be supplied. 'Night and day we pray most earnestly that we may see you again and supply what is lacking in your faith' (3:10). It becomes clear that one of the great marks of real assurance is the 'more and more' aspect of discipleship, which Paul now begins to stress at chapter 4:1, the pivot between the two halves of the letter. 'Finally, brothers, we instructed you how to live in order to please God, as in fact you are living' – chapters 1 to 3. 'Now we ask and urge you in the Lord Jesus to do this more and more' – chapters 4 and 5.

Confident Christian assurance is not simply looking back at what has been, but moving forward in 'more and more' of the same. Such progress does not move forward into something different; it is working at the same gospel more and more in the lives of those who responded to it, the aspect of discipleship which is at the heart of the last two chapters. No creed is secure unless it is believed without reservation. No virtue is safe if it is not passionate. In the same way, no past reputation is a guarantee of present reality. Unless the distinctive marks of Christian faith are developing more and more, then even though we might look back with enormous thanksgiving, we would have to look forward with trepidation. It is only as gospel qualities are developing more and more that the church is really an authentic church. That is how you know that the real gospel has come, 'in the power of the Holy Spirit and in deep conviction' (1:5). It is when people turn their back on their idols and start to serve the living and true God, and when the perspective of the last day, waiting for Jesus, becomes the dominant concern of how they live in the present. That is the mark of the Holy Spirit at work in deep conviction. It is when, however difficult and testing the present proves to be, whatever suffering it produces, the believers keep on believing and hoping 'more and more', keep on loving the Lord and one another 'more and more', because they know that the present persecution is as nothing compared with the coming wrath. It is because they have got their perspective right about the eternal realities, that they are able to follow in the footsteps of a Christ who suffered, who went through that suffering to glory, and so to live out the theology of the cross.

These apostolic assurances of spiritual reality are equally important to us in our generation. When someone asks you, 'I'm not really sure – have I really become a Christian?' If you are in Thessalonians you would ask, 'Is chapter 1 true of you? Are there evidences in your life of the faith which verses 9 and 10 talk about? Can you see anything of love that labours and a hope that endures?' Or if someone is wondering, 'Was I really taught the truth? Have I got the real gospel or is there something else that I ought to be believing?' Paul would say, 'Did you see the characteristics of chapters 2 and 3 lived out in the messenger and are you now living the same way? Have those who taught you the gospel you believe in demonstrated that godliness of character and are you following in their footsteps?' Paul's message to the Thessalonians is not that they are a perfect church, needing nothing. How could that ever be true of any church in this world? His message to them is, 'You are authentic; rejoice in it and prove it by being more and more authentic, growing "more and more" in faith, love and hope.' Real gospel work is verified by the simple fact that its converts live in order to please God. That is the bottom line, the fundamental reality (4:1).

5

A Life that Pleases
1 Thessalonians 4:1-12

[1]Finally, brothers, we instructed you how to live in order to please God, as in fact you are living. Now we ask you and urge you in the Lord Jesus to do this more and more. [2]For you know what instructions we gave you by the authority of the Lord Jesus.

[3]It is God's will that you should be sanctified: that you should avoid sexual immorality; [4]that each of you should learn to control his own body in a way that is holy and honourable, [5]not in passionate lust like the heathen, who do not know God; [6]and that in this matter no-one should wrong his brother or take advantage of him. The Lord will punish men for all such sins, as we have already told you and warned you. [7]For God did not call us to be impure, but to live a holy life. [8]Therefore, he who rejects this instruction does not reject man but God, who gives you his Holy Spirit.

[9]Now about brotherly love we do not need to write to you, for you yourselves have been taught by God to love each other. [10]And in fact, you do love all the brothers throughout Macedonia. Yet we urge you, brothers, to do so more and more.

[11]Make it your ambition to lead a quiet life, to mind your own business and to work with your hands, just as we told you, [12]so that your daily life may win the respect of outsiders and so that you will not be dependent on anybody (1 Thess. 4:1-12).

This is very clearly the start of the second half of the letter. Wanamaker observes that chapters 2 and 3 re-establish and confirm the relationship of loving brotherly concern between Paul and the church, which now becomes the basis for the exhortation following in chapters 4 and 5.[1] We might also observe that from verse 1 to verse 3a, there is a deepening intensity of concern and constraint. Verse 1 picks up the continuity theme. 'The instructions you received from me when I was with you were in no way deficient,' says Paul, 'and neither was your obedience to them. You received my word as the word of God, not the word of men, and that is a guarantee of the Spirit's work in you.'

Practical instruction must always follow gospel preaching, so here the specific evidences of gospel living will be spelt out. Paul uses his favourite description of the Christian life. He describes it as a 'walk' (although the NIV translates it 'live'), so appropriate for the concept of continuing on the same pathway of reality, one step at a time. You have set out on the walk, so keep on walking in that direction, in order to please God. Walk more and more that way. That is the message. Biblical spirituality is neither a roller-coaster ride, nor is it a journey of dramatic U-turns. Where the Word of God is being taught, biblical spirituality consists of a long obedience in the same direction. But Paul is not hesitant to press home this point, asking and urging them to 'abound' or 'excel'. That, surely, is the right sort of possibility thinking. It is the spiritual equivalent of 'the sky's the limit!' There is to be no limit to our growing faith, and love and hope, even in this present world.

By verse 2, the exhortation is strengthened to a command. 'For you know what instructions' – it is a word used of military orders – 'we gave you by the authority of the Lord Jesus.' So by dominical authority, issued in the Lord's name, with the requirement of obedience, Paul backs up what he is about to say to them. And the final thrust is in verse 3a, where the exhortation which became a command, now becomes the will of God: 'It is the will of God that you should be sanctified.' That statement is totally unambiguous. What pleases God is that which is in accordance with his will, namely that his people should be set apart as his special property and for his exclusive use, sanctified.

It is important to stop here for a moment and look at the logic of this, so that we can see why Paul stresses holiness so much in this letter. Remember this was the climax of his prayer in 3:13: 'May he strengthen your hearts so that you will be blameless and holy in the presence of our God and Father, when our Lord Jesus comes with all his holy ones.' Of course, for Paul, for those Jews who had been converted, and indeed for those God-fearing Greeks, attracted originally to the synagogue, the Old Testament background was both vivid and significant. We are familiar with the refrain that runs through the books of Moses, especially Leviticus, 'Be holy, because I am holy, says the Lord.' However, the additional information that is given to expound that refrain is highly significant. For example, Leviticus 20:8 states, 'Keep my decrees and follow them. I am the LORD who sanctifies you.' So 'being holy as I am holy' is not just *our* response or responsibility, it is the will of *God* being worked out by God – 'I am the Lord who sets you apart as holy'.

In contemporary Christianity we tend to narrow the term 'holiness' to the context of moral purity, as indicative of God's righteousness. Certainly it is being used here in this context against the background of pagan sexual immorality, but it is a deeper and more foundational term than that. In biblical thinking, holiness is not just an attribute of God, along with other attributes. It is much more descriptive of the essential being of God, in all his transcendent otherness. The characteristic way in which that is described in Scripture is by God being called holy. In his book, *Distinctive Ideas of the Old Testament*, N. Snaith writes, 'Holiness is the most intimately divine word of all. It has to do with the very Nature of Deity.'[2] Or again, as another Old Testament scholar puts it, 'Holiness expresses the idea of God. Holy is not a word that expresses an attribute of deity, but deity *itself*. Not *what* God is, but *that* he is.'[3] We need to rehabilitate the whole biblical range of the concept of holiness. Obviously, central to its meaning is the idea of separation, but we tend to use that mainly negatively. When we talk about separation, we ask separation from what or other than what? Biblical holiness expresses this positive fact of the divine nature: that God is, in himself, other. Therefore, holiness in the people of God, who is utterly righteous and pure, splendid in his majesty and in his own being, must consist in being set apart for him.

This is how we might begin to recover the biblical essence of holiness from the bad press the word has had, due to phrases like 'holier than thou'. Holiness describes the very essence of the divine being and becomes the very purpose for which he has brought us into union with him. When we rejoice in being separated to God, there is nothing negative in that. It is what God is continually doing in his people, making us like him. That is why in verse 3a it is God's will, it is God's very purpose, that you should be sanctified.

This helps us to see why holiness is so central to Thessalonians. The whole purpose of Old Testament law was that the covenant people might know how to live to please God, although of course, their sinful nature meant that they could not do it. That is why the sacrificial system was built into the law. For us, as new covenant people, knowing that Christ has not destroyed the law, but fulfilled it, it is 'the authority of the Lord Jesus' (4:2) which commands us to live in a way that pleases God, as the indication of gospel reality in our lives. Only the Lord Jesus could claim always to do the things that please the Father on earth, which was the outward sign that he really was who he claimed to be. That is why he could offer that pure and perfect will on the cross as a substitute for our rebellious wills. It set him apart. We know that Jesus is the Son of God, not only by the miracles, but by his character, the sheer holiness of Jesus, his 'otherness'. This is the great strand of evidence that proves that he really is God.

Sexual morality

What then will be the mark of gospel reality in the lives of Christ's people, whether in Thessalonica or in our world today? Holiness. New life in Christ is only authenticated and recognised by Christ-like characteristics. Set-apartness from the behaviour patterns of the pagan culture is one mark of that reality, but it is a set-apartness to cultivate godliness. For God to do that, for it is his will to sanctify us, is the other mark of that reality. But if our view of the Christian life is basically centred around 'me' and 'my' enjoyment of the blessings of the gospel, without any consistent moral and spiritual challenge to holiness, we are missing one of the great marks of reality, which ought to provide a cutting edge for the gospel in a pagan society.

Verses 3-8 explore this in the area of sexual morality. Paul immediately spells out the general concept in more explicit terms. What is practical holiness? It is sexual purity. That isn't all it is, but it must certainly be expressed in this way – 'that you should avoid sexual immorality' (v. 3b). The Greek word is *porneia*, which means sexual sin in its widest sense. In Old Testament times, when the conflict with paganism was often drawn in the starkest terms, idolatry and immorality clearly went hand in hand. The same was certainly true in first century Greece – the one legitimised the other. So having turned from idols (1:9) the Thessalonians might be tempted back to the temples and shrines which denied the objective reality of the true and living God, and that might be a problem for them. But it would be much easier still to slip back into the pagan immorality which licensed prostitution, often in the name of religion, and turned a blind eye to lust, much as our neo-pagan society today increasingly does. So Paul spells the will of God out in specific detail.

In the verses that follow, there are two problem areas. They are not very difficult to identify or define. They are 'passionate lust' (v. 5) and 'wronging one's brother' (v. 6). But before we come to those, we need to look at verse 4, because there is a footnote to the text which introduces us to a discussion about its meaning: 'that each of you should learn to control his own body, in a way that is holy and honourable'. The RSV, along with other translations, including the footnote in the NIV, have as an alternative the translation 'learn to live with his own wife', 'learn to acquire a wife' or 'take a wife'. So we have here two alternatives. Does Paul mean 'to take a wife' or 'to control his own body'? The noun concerned is *skuos* which means, literally, a vessel, a utensil or tool. In Greek thought, the body is the *skuos* of the soul; it is the vessel in which the soul resides. But the verb clearly means 'to gain' or 'to acquire' which hardly fits with 'body' – you can hardly gain or acquire your body, unless it means to acquire control over. On the other hand, the verb does fit well with a wife – you can acquire a wife – and *skuos* is used in that context in 1 Peter 3:7, where the wife is referred to as the weaker 'vessel'. Whichever meaning is selected, whether Paul is talking about self-control, or about honourable Christian marriage, the emphasis is on the Christian's attitude towards God – we are to be holy – and to others, we are to be honourable. Clearly, it is the knowledge of God and what it is to live in a way that pleases him which delivers from passionate lust, because the characteristic of the pagans, who are indulging in passionate lust, is that they do not know God (v. 5). To know God means to turn my back on that way of living. Real gospel work, then, is proved by a change in sexual behaviour. Just as Romans 1 teaches that the pagan suppresses the knowledge of God in order that his moral behaviour can remain unchanged, in a similar way, if I have a true knowledge of God, it will be seen in the way I behave sexually.

At this point, verse 6 adds the other distinctively Christian ingredient of brotherly love. 'In this matter (of sexual morality), no one should wrong his brother or take advantage of him.' Knowledge of God – faith – leads to love for the family of God which is created by the faith of the gospel. So the new community, the flagship church of Thessalonica, must not allow its message to be denied by sexual behaviour which, literally, 'oversteps the mark' or claims more than one is entitled to. But what does that mean in practice? Sadly, some of the

contemporary cults illustrate only too easily how that can happen.
When the word of God is not ruling, holiness will not be the
goal, and then all sorts of 'overstepping the mark' – wife-
swapping, sharing partners, adultery and fornication – will
follow. They may be given spiritual names, and justified by all
sorts of pseudo-revelation and special pleading, but such
behaviour is both a great offence against the holiness of God,
and also a great offence against brotherly love. If sin like that is
tolerated in the church, it will lead to a blurring of the distinctions
which separate sanctified believers from their pagan neighbours,
and it will lead to all sorts of internal jealousies, strife and
fragmentation. This remains a very important central issue still,
and explains why the morality of the church today and discipline
within the church to preserve these biblical standards are
essential for gospel work to continue.

God's discipline

After applying the logic, Paul now applies the sanctions. Clearly,
he had already done this in Thessalonica as part of his original
discipleship programme, but this is now repeated with great force
and seriousness. 'The Lord will punish men for all such sins, as
we have already told you and warned you' (v. 6b). The subject
matter provides the tone. In fact, Paul uses the ultimate sanction
– the Lord Jesus is a punisher of all such sins. We live in a
culture that does not want to hear that. It wants to hear that the
Lord Jesus understands my temptations and condones my sins.
But Paul says the Lord Jesus is a punisher of all such sins. The
will of God for our sanctification (v. 3) is confirmed by the call
of God (v. 7): God did not call us to be impure, but to live a holy
life. Notice how Paul includes himself in the picture. He is
underlining the moral separation and the distinctive difference
of the new community. God's call picks us out; it really does
separate us from the rest of humanity. For what purpose? First,
we have the negative, 'not to uncleanness', because that is the
characteristic of the environment we are called from. Then, we

have the positive – to live a holy life. It is the same word as in verse 3, to be sanctified.

Let us summarise the teaching. God's call in the gospel brings us into the sphere of God's will, which is to make us like himself, holy. If this is God's plan, then one of the signs of reality is that we are motivated to co-operate with him in that great project, and that we acknowledge that this is a priority for our churches. Keep the corporate context in view. He is not simply talking to us as individuals, though of course that is true, but we must remember the plurals that come all the way through this letter. It has a corporate church application. Consequently, verse 8, states that he who rejects this instruction, that is, the general instruction of sexual morality, does not reject man, but God.

Then notice this lovely phrase at the end of the verse, 'who gives you his Holy Spirit'. To reject the command to holiness is to reject not only the God who calls, but also the God who equips, through the gift of the Spirit, the One who is holy and who makes us holy. The verb, 'to reject', means to treat something as null and void, to bring it to nothing, to frustrate its purpose. The meaning is clear and plain. If, in the church you allow people to go back to sexual immorality, to choose against the character of God, out of self-indulgence, that immorality is evidence of an idolatry that has taken root in their hearts, for God's call is to live a holy life. If you reject that call, then you reject God. And if you reject God, then you grieve, quench and nullify the work of the Spirit of holiness, whom God has given to you in order to enable you to live that holy life. That is to deny the very heart and purpose of the gospel.

I am impressed both by how strong the language is, and by the fact that Paul sees this as a number one problem. It is the very first thing he corrects. The hint is clearly there in the time he devoted during his visit to teaching and warning on this area. There must have been a real problem surfacing which Timothy has reported. Perhaps verse 6 is a hint of this – 'as we have already told you and warned' about these sins which are beginning to appear. Pagan laxity may have been Christianised among believers in the church. Perhaps some of them were being encouraged to write this part of Paul's teaching off as some kind of hangover from his Jewish legalism – a rule taught by man. But in fact, Paul argues, it is at the heart of God's instructions and purposes for gospel people. The indwelling Holy Spirit who has created the new community is a sign of the age to come. Its characteristic will be that God's people will be perfectly in God's likeness. That is another reason why the emphasis on the parousia runs through the letter highlighting 'that you may be blameless and holy in the presence of our God and Father, when our Lord Jesus comes' (3:13). If you lose that end-point then you are not going to worry much about morality now. You will be able to say, 'Oh that doesn't matter! God understands! The times are different!'

Or look at 1 Thessalonians 5:23: 'May God himself, the God of peace, sanctify you through and through. May your whole spirit, soul and body be kept blameless at the coming of our Lord Jesus Christ.' If that is the end-point to which we are moving, as it clearly is, then holiness cannot be an optional extra. The process has to be going on, all the time, now. We all need that reminder in our relativistic tolerance. We need to tell ourselves and our churches that fornication and adultery are still grievous sins that mar the body of Christ and deny the gospel, that passionate lust and whatever feeds it is heathenish, and calls out the righteous wrath of God. We need to reaffirm that celibacy outside of marriage and fidelity within it are still the only ways to reflect the character of our God of faithful commitment, in his steadfast love to his people. Nothing else is holy or honourable in the eyes of such a God. If we know him at all, we shall know that.

But the warnings are here, precisely because of the danger. So we shouldn't be surprised at either the devil's attack on us, or our own vulnerability on this front. This is where the gospel actually cuts into the culture. Chapter 5:8 will teach us 'since we belong to the day, let us be self-controlled, putting on faith and love as a breastplate, and the hope of salvation as a helmet'.

To lower the moral standards in the name of love, or to pretend that such sins no longer exist, or no longer require church discipline, is to make the church the laughing-stock of the world and the object of God's judgment.

Brotherly love

If verses 3-8 explain the prayer of 3:13 – 'that you will be blameless and holy in the presence of our God and Father when our Lord Jesus comes with all his holy ones' – then verses 9-12 seem to have the same function regarding the prayer of 3:12: 'May the Lord make your love increase and overflow for each other and for everyone else, just as ours does for you.' The point is stated clearly in verse 9: 'Now about brotherly love we do not need to write to you, for you yourselves have been taught by God to love each other. And in fact, you do love all the brothers throughout Macedonia. Yet we urge you, brothers, to do so more and more.' So the 'more and more' principle applies as much to love as to faith and holiness.

The phrase 'we do not need to write to you' is generally seen as a rhetorical convention, by which the readers are first being confirmed in what they are already doing right. This then becomes the basis of an exhortation to continue in this course of action and to develop it even further. We can recognise an effective pastoral methodology in this. Everyone thrives on encouragement! But Paul's purpose is to encourage the Thessalonian believers in their assurance. He wants them to understand that the brotherly love *(philadelphia)* which already characterises their new community is irrefutable evidence that they have been 'taught by God' (v. 9). The term 'taught-by-God' *(theodidaktos)* is a word specially coined by Paul for use here. But if it is an invented word, the concept has an important Old Testament background, on which is built a significant New Testament application.

The Old Testament root can be traced back to Isaiah 54:13. You may remember that Isaiah 54 constitutes the commentary on the great Suffering Servant song of Isaiah 53. After the song comes the explanation of what will spring from the Servant's work, one of the fruits of which is detailed in verse 13: 'All your sons will be 'theodidaktos' – taught by the Lord – and great will be your children's peace.' In other words, Isaiah is teaching that one of the great characteristics of the coming age of salvation will be that God's people are personally taught by him. No longer is the law to be written on tablets of stone, but written on the heart. Paul is stressing again this mark of gospel authenticity – you have been taught this by God. 'This love that you are demonstrating is not something that I have put into you, or that you have decided to exercise. You have been taught it by God and he has generated it in you.' The same idea is present in John's Gospel where in Jesus' dialogue with the Jews, following the feeding of the five thousand, he says: 'It is written in the Prophets: "They will all be taught by God." Everyone who listens to the Father and learns from him comes to me. No-one has seen the Father except the one who is from God; only he has seen the Father. I tell you the truth, he who believes has everlasting life. I am the bread of life' (John 6:45-48). So to be taught by the Father is to come to the Son, to receive everlasting life.

That background helps to make Paul's point doubly clear. The gospel is the means by which God's people are taught by him. They have entered into the blessings of salvation, the Spirit is within them writing the law on their hearts, and they have believed in the Son, the bread of life, who has brought them to the Father. Only the gospel of the Lord Jesus can both teach and enable us to practise this life-changing principle – to love each other. Such love is the mark of gospel reality, which is what separates Christians as distinctive from the pagan culture around them. Only divine power can produce that change, which is why it is an irrefutable proof of spiritual reality.

Our danger, however, is that instead of judging spiritual effectiveness by the distinctives which the Bible teaches us, we judge it by worldly standards. Trying to squeeze us into its mould, the world tempts us to judge our effectiveness as Christians by whether we are performing according to its own cultural criteria.

The annual 'preacher of the year' competition run by *The Times* newspaper is an interesting example of this prevailing trend. Firstly, it introduces a worldly mechanism, the award of prizes or 'oscars' into a spiritual activity. But from the world's point of view, a preacher is much like any other public performer – actor, novelist or pop star. They are all 'communicators'. Next, the sermon is judged by those criteria which are applied to other forms of public entertainment, so that it is neutralised and completely held captive by the culture. A recent 'winner' was commended by the assessors for four things in his preaching which secured the prize. His sermon was 'committed, exciting, humorous and poignant'. It could have been the Booker prize for fiction. There is nothing about biblical content or spiritual effectiveness; it wouldn't be considered. The point was made explicit in the same edition of the paper, where in its third leader on 'pulpit prizes', preaching is described as 'an oratorical art in decline'. The reason given is that sound-bites and interviews have replaced the monologue. Also, people are embarrassed by the hierarchy symbolised in the pulpit, twelve feet above contradiction (it used to be six!), and congregations have more calls on their time than when the sermon was the only intelligent argument they were likely to hear all week. The other revealing comment in the leader is that the preachers in the competition are commended because they 'cited authorities from Julian of Norwich to Mother Teresa and Mr. Spock, and deployed parable, homily, personal witness, anecdote, emotion, body language and all the other aspects of an art that stretches back to the Old Testament prophets and the early Christian fathers'. What is the purpose of the competition? 'To encourage the art and to bring to wider notice those who have the rare talent of preaching but gain little public attention outside their churches.'

Is that not a revealing example of how our culture judges the church? The world is saying to the church, 'Perform within our criteria. If you are any good, we will give you some public attention outside your church. You could become "preacher of the year"!' When we have Christian media personalities whose

shows outstrip those of the culture in terms of popularity, as
some do in the States, then the world will say that the church is
really doing the job. When it is more exciting to go to church
than to go to a pop-concert, then we shall really impact the
younger generation. When our knowledge is deeper, or our
mystical experience is more moving, or our worship more
aesthetic than what is on offer in the world, then the crowds will
really come flocking in.

But, the Bible does not talk in those terms. It talks about
something as mundane and down-to-earth as increasing brotherly
love being the mark of reality. Our great danger is that we shall
start to behave in the way we are expected to behave. We start
to take on the culture's critique, to react to it, because we want
above all things to be relevant, but we do forget the subversive-
ness of our gospel. Its power lies precisely in the fact that it
does not dance to the world's tune. We march to a different
drum-beat. Paul's answer would be that none of the world's
criteria can judge biblical spirituality, but that when a group of
heterogeneous people in a local congregation start loving one
another, because they are obeying God's word, living holy lives
because his Holy Spirit is at work in them, there you have
something that no human organisation or programme could
possibly produce. That is the proof that God is at work. And
such love cannot be contained within one local community; it
must spread. 'You love all the brothers, throughout the whole
province, throughout Macedonia' (v. 10).

This love is a practical target of godliness that we can pray
for and work at, as a visible mark of spiritual reality. We do not
need recognition outside of our own churches in terms of the
media graciously giving us exposure. What we need is for 'more
and more' Christian love impacting hundreds and thousands of
lives all around the country. So the 'more and more' extends
geographically as well as in intensity and depth, but we need to
be urged to practise it. We have the moral and spiritual
responsibility to make every effort to develop this love, which
is why our fellowship across the denominations is so important.

Gospel unity must transcend the denominational barriers which will always be, by definition, of secondary importance. It is vital that our understanding of other Christian believers, who do not share our distinctive traditions, should increase, so that our love for one another, as members of the one family of God, can grow. We need to be supporting one another in practical ways, praying for each other, strengthening one another in gospel work, increasingly concerned for one another's well-being, rather than competing with one another. The Thessalonians seem to have taken the lead in pioneering fellowship between the believers throughout Greece. It was a wonderful indication that God was at work in them.

As the section closes, verses 11 and 12 are clearly angled at the threat they are facing. Both grammatically and in thought content, they belong to verses 9 and 10, because the verb, 'we urge you' (*parakaleo*) has four infinitives that depend on it. We urge you to do so more and more (v. 10), to aspire to live quietly, to mind your own affairs, to work with your own hands (v. 11). It seems reasonable to recognize the last three as practical examples of the first. This is what it means to live a life of brotherly love.

However, closer examination of verse 11 may strike us as being a rather strange example. A little more of the Thessalonian context is a help here. It seems beyond doubt that Paul has in view those whom he later calls 'the idle' (5:14). There is a deliberate contrast at the start of verse 11 in the form of an oxymoron, like 'bitter-sweet'. Literally it reads 'seek restlessly to be still', or 'strive to be calm'. Clearly, he wants to grab their attention. From what he later writes, we know that there was a good deal of excitement and heightened expectation in the church about the nearness of the day of the Lord, which was having an unsettling effect. People seem to have opted out of work for super-spiritual reasons. They wanted to attend to the Lord's business, they wanted to prepare the way for the coming King, so they couldn't, or wouldn't, do their daily work. In a culture where people were paid daily, they would very soon become dependent on the goodwill and generosity of others. But that is directly contrary, Paul says, to what he taught and practised. In 2:9, he told them, 'you remember, brothers, our toil and hardship. We worked night and day in order not to be a burden to anyone while we preached the gospel of God to you.' So he says, in verse 11, 'Make it your ambition to lead a quiet life ... just as we told you.'

At this point, it will be helpful to take a brief excursion into 2 Thessalonians where we can see more clearly what was happening. 2 Thessalonians 3:11 reads: 'We hear that some among you are idle. They are not busy; they are busy-bodies. Such people we command and urge in the Lord Jesus Christ to settle down and earn the bread they eat.' Their free time made them meddlers; they became busybodies. But how could that be an expression of brotherly love? Their refusal to work made them dependent on others which the next verse points out is wrong. They should earn the bread they eat. Returning to our passage, we are not surprised to find that the reaction of outsiders is a very important constraint (v. 12). We can reconstruct the situation. If these idle people sponge on the brotherly love of others, to the extent that they 'feel led' to be supported by the financial gifts of others within the church, the outsiders will have no respect for such parasites, and they will have precious little respect for the gullibility of their fellow-Christians who are actually supporting them. The whole credibility of the gospel is at stake here. To support oneself and one's family through one's work must always be a Christian aim; it is an expression of love. Of course, those who are unable to work, through sickness or injury, or today through unemployment, are in a different category. Brotherly love will naturally want to support the destitute; but not the idle.

Again, it is important to see how this apparently mundane normality is Paul's goal. The gospel has constituted them as a separate community – that is God's will, expressed in his call. But it is not a call either to eccentricity or to gullibility. To be eagerly expecting the coming of the Lord does not require

believers to leave their jobs or cease to support their families –
quite the opposite. <u>The watching world is not hugely impressed
by emotional hype and extremism, but it is attracted by ordinary
people, living ordinary lives, who demonstrate an extraordinary
godliness, seen in love</u>. And we must keep saying that to
ourselves and one another, so as to keep believing it, praying it
and living it. What wins the world's respect, ultimately, is that
same mark of genuineness which proves a real gospel work of
God is going on in the congregation.

There is a concluding pastoral application for congregational
life today in our local churches. We have seen the necessity to
develop holiness and brotherly love 'more and more', and every
member has a part to play in that. But do we encourage one
another sufficiently when we see the genuine marks of the Holy
Spirit at work among us? Pushing for higher standards can sometimes come across as somewhat critical and negative. We do
need to learn from Paul's commendations and we need to use
them as the basis for a ministry of encouragement, because that,
after all, is the work of the Holy Spirit, the Paraclete. It is nothing about being wishy-washy or tolerating sin, as we have seen
very clearly. Sin has to be confronted and exposed, but we are
to be motivated always by love. When we know we are loved,
we are able to receive from people things that would otherwise
be hard to hear and might produce great resistance. Paul is not
buttering them up. He is simply sharing the genuine love he has
for them, knowing that this love, reciprocated in their love overflowing for him, is the great mark of the gospel. That cannot be
fabricated any other way. It means that in our truth communication we are always to be people-orientated. We are always seeking to build up, to strengthen, to increase that brotherly love
between us. It has been wisely said that congregations are not
passive buckets to be pumped into. No, they are precious, but
fragile, redeemed sinners like ourselves, who need every ounce
of love and encouragement we can give them. To do that 'more
and more', says Paul, is to live in a way that is pleasing to God,
because that demonstrates the authenticity of his gospel.

6

A Hope that Endures (1)
1 Thessalonians 4:13-18

[13]Brothers, we do not want you to be ignorant about those who fall asleep, or to grieve like the rest of men, who have no hope. [14]We believe that Jesus died and rose again and so we believe that God will bring with Jesus those who have fallen asleep in him. [15]According to the Lord's own word, we tell you that we who are still alive, who are left till the coming of the Lord, will certainly not precede those who have fallen asleep. [16]For the Lord himself will come down from heaven, with a loud command, with the voice of the archangel and with the trumpet call of God, and the dead in Christ will rise first. [17]After that, we who are still alive and are left will be caught up together with them in the clouds to meet the Lord in the air. And so we will be with the Lord for ever. [18]Therefore encourage each other with these words (1 Thess. 4:13-18)

We move now into the major doctrinal or teaching section of the letter, as Paul turns from faith and love to hope, and to this great theme of the coming of the Lord. The section is clearly in two parts (4:13-18 and 5:1-11), divided by the chapter division for us, each ending with an exhortation to encouragement: 'Therefore encourage each other with these words' (4:18) and 'Therefore encourage one another and build each other up, just as in fact you are doing' (5:11).

The first section deals with a particular question that was troubling the Thessalonian Christians: What happens to Christians who die, before the Lord comes? Then the second section stresses that the timing of the parousia cannot be known, but that what matters is readiness. And Paul teaches them, and us, what that means in practical down-to-earth terms. Both sections are considerably elaborated in the second letter, with material that we do not have anywhere else in the New Testament, so we will use that to develop our understanding as the exposition proceeds.

Undoubtedly, the expectation of the Lord's return, was a much stronger, more prominent ingredient in Christian thinking and living in the early church, and especially in Thessalonica, than it is in the contemporary church. We have already seen that the idea of the parousia is not so much the 'second' coming, but the 'coming', the day when the King arrives in all his glory to judge and to reward. It is the coming which determines Paul's own life and ministry in so many ways. Remember how in 1:10 he describes the Christian life as waiting for Jesus. Our problem is that 'waiting' sounds inactive and boring to us. We even have waiting rooms at doctors' practices and dentists' surgeries and railway stations, which are not places most of us relish. Waiting rooms tends to have very negative connotations. But this biblical waiting is highly active. It is turning to serve the living and true God (1:9). Clearly, there was a much greater sense of urgency in this, if the coming of the Lord could be at any time.

We live, by contrast, at the end of 1900 years, when as Peter predicted, scoffers have come saying, 'Where is this "coming" he promised? Ever since our fathers died, everything goes on as it has since the beginning of creation' (2 Peter 3:4). Naturally, we feel the effect of that. In some ways, it is inevitable. We do not doubt the reality of the Lord's return, it is the final point on our doctrinal basis, or it is a sentence that we say every Sunday in the creed, but we are not usually animated by a daily expectation of its imminence. So we do have to do some thinking to get back to Thessalonica where excitement levels seem to have been high. We do not normally think that our waiting and serving could end tomorrow. If we really did, it might focus our minds wonderfully. We are more used to calculating the number of years to our retirement. But for Paul it was a much more urgent matter, and one that had huge impact on his present priorities and experience. We can see that in a cross-reference from much later in his ministry, where he addresses this whole matter in the letter to Titus. Towards the end of his ministry and still reflecting on the centrality of the coming, Paul writes: 'For the grace of God that brings salvation has appeared to all men. It teaches us to say "No" to ungodliness and worldly passions, and to live self-controlled, upright and godly lives in this present age, while we wait for the blessed hope – the glorious appearing of our great God and Saviour, Jesus Christ, who gave himself for us to redeem us from all wickedness and to purify for himself a people that are his very own, eager to do what is good' (Titus 2:11-14).

What does waiting for the blessed hope, for the coming, actually mean? Saying 'No' to ungodliness, living self-controlled, upright and godly lives in this present age. That is the present purpose of our eternal redemption. While it is true that completion is found only in the 'not yet' dimension of the glory of God in heaven, nevertheless the whole emphasis is that the process is operating now. The present purpose of redemption is to produce a purified, holy people, eager to do what is good, to which the certainty and suddenness of the parousia was undoubtedly a powerful motivator in the early church. If the Lord Jesus is going to return suddenly, then I want to know how to live in a way that is pleasing to him at his coming. I want to be found holy and blameless in the presence of our God and Father when the Lord Jesus comes with his holy ones.

Christian grieving over death

But what was going on in Thessalonica? Verse 13 indicates that there was ignorance about those who had fallen asleep, or perhaps about those who might fall asleep. Deaths may well have occurred since the church had been founded. Most scholars think the letter is within about a year of its foundation, so it is quite possible that more than one may have died in that time. This is more likely than speculation about what will happen if someone dies, because of the comment about the grief that is produced. Paul does not want them to grieve without hope, because such grieving would be indistinguishable from that of the pagans. In the context of 4:1, that cannot be pleasing to God. Hope is one of the great characteristics of Christian reality, and we saw right at the start of the letter that it is the factor which produces perseverance and endurance (1:3). If there is no hope in the church, there will be no perseverance, and no perseverance will mean the sinking of the flagship church and the consequent demise of the gospel in Greece.

It seems likely that Timothy has reported back to Paul that this is an area which is 'lacking in their faith', and so Paul sets out to address it head-on. He knows that it is only the eschatological perspective that will keep the church going through its suffering, since it is the future outcome that makes sense of the present pain. He is encouraging them to continue to be a high profile community (an inference we can legitimately draw from 4:12) because he wants their daily lives to be known and observed. There is not the slightest indication that retreating into a Christian ghetto is a viable option for the Thessalonian church. But let us put ourselves in their shoes! If you think that being a high profile Christian is going to lead to suffering, and perhaps even to death, then it makes you stop and think, doesn't it? Further, if you wonder whether those who have died already are not actually at a great disadvantage, because they will not be here when the parousia occurs, you might then decide that it would be healthier all round to merge quietly into the background, not to be so distinctive in your lifestyle and to do your waiting for Jesus in the privacy of your own home. In other words you would be tempted to go low-key and low-profile, rather like the sign over a 'drive-in' church in the USA – 'Worship God in the privacy of your own automobile.'

To come out of the public arena into a private piety is always tempting when the heat is on, but of course it is never an option in New Testament thinking. To have wrong views about the parousia, and about the impact of death on one's experience of it, could spell disaster in terms of the witness and perseverance of the church. That is why Paul is not prepared to allow their ignorance to continue.

The other emphasis which is very Thessalonian is the contrast between the believers and the 'rest of men', which verse 13 makes. Part of the assurance that Paul is trying to build in to them throughout the letter is that they really are different. That is one of the great marks of gospel reality. The severe persecution they are under is generated by the fact that they believe in another King, one Jesus. Their working faith, their labouring love and their persevering hope are all explicable only in terms of the gospel. They are a new community; they have turned, they are serving and waiting. They have totally different reference points, because they see the parousia of the Lord Jesus as the climactic fulfilment, to which they are moving. They are utterly different from the 'rest of men' and so are we. Already they live in the life of eternity while the 'rest of men' are time-bound. They are to be alert and self-controlled, as chapter 5 will say, while others are asleep or drunk. They are sons of the light and of the day, while others live in the darkness and night. These contrasts are fully developed in 5:4-8. The point is that the believer's attitude to death is another distinguishing feature which witnesses to the reality of the gospel. If we are looking at cutting-edges of the gospel, they are seen in the difference of Christians from the world around them – in holiness, brotherly love and in their view of death and what lies beyond. That is what Paul begins now to spell out.

Of course, Christians grieve over the loss of loved ones. Verse 13 does not say that we do not grieve, though we may have met Christians who take it that way, usually with devastating results. They bottle up their grief, refusing to acknowledge it, and we all know the pastoral problems that result. No, Christians do grieve because of the pain of the parting and the severance of the relationship, and it is right that we should, but what is not pleasing to God is if we grieve as those who have no hope. That is to say, we do not so grieve for the loved one who is a believer, because for them their present now and all their future is hope fulfilled. To know that transforms even our present experience of grieving, as Paul spells out in the following verses.

In many ways verse 14 is the key. 'We believe that Jesus died and rose again and so we believe that God will bring with Jesus those who have fallen asleep in him.' Meditating on this statement, I have come to see how very remarkable it is. Paul is saying that our hope for the future is grounded in the certainty of the past. That is both very Christian and very different from contemporary culture, but here we are given the reason why Christian grieving is not hopeless. The structure of the verse is that of a logical argument – if we believe A, then we believe B. It follows that one leads to the other. We believe that Jesus died and rose again, but not just in the sense of believing it as an historical fact. He could have written, 'We know that Jesus died and rose again.' It *is* an historical fact. But Paul uses the word 'believe' because faith is the essence of the gospel. Further, the emphasis here is on the resurrection – we believe that Jesus died *and rose again.* Now the parallelism of the verse is Jesus died – Christians die; Jesus rose – Christians rise. That would seem to be the obvious implication, but he does not actually balance the sentence that way. He does not say that because we believe that Jesus died and rose again, we believe that those who died in Jesus will rise again. Rather, he balances the sentence by saying,

'So we believe that God will bring with Jesus those who have fallen asleep in him.' The resurrection is not the fundamental issue here. The question is rather what is the relationship of Christians who have died to the parousia.

We should also notice how the change in description between verses 13 and 14 is significant. In verse 13, Christians who have died are called literally 'the sleeping ones'. It is a present participle, by which Paul means obviously those who have died. That is not an exclusively Christian way of speaking about death. The Old Testament talks of sleeping with our fathers, and the idea occurs in secular Greek too that death is sleep. But it was especially taken up by Christians, because the key thing about being asleep is that you will awake. If you are asleep and you are not going to awake, then you are truly dead!

However, in verse 14, the aorist tense of the same verb is used, referring to the moment of death, so the sleeping ones are those who died, or literally 'fell asleep through Jesus'. The usual translation 'in him' is perhaps better rendered 'through him'. If they fell asleep in, or through, Jesus, then God will bring them with Jesus. The first ingredient of the hope that transforms grief is that those who have fallen asleep in Jesus are in the immediate presence of God, they are with Jesus. That is why he can bring them. It is also why Paul can say elsewhere: 'I desire to depart and be with Christ, which is better by far' (Phil. 1:23), or again 'We would prefer to be away from the body and at home with the Lord' (2 Cor. 5:8).

No unbeliever could say that in either first century Greece or in twentieth century Britain. No one would prefer to be away from the body unless he knew that it meant being at home with the Lord. If there was any belief in an afterlife in Greece at that time, it was, at best, a shadowy existence in Hades. The dead were often called 'the shades'. It was very different from the full-blooded life on earth. F. F. Bruce quotes Catullus on this. He says in one of his poems, 'The sun can set and rise again, but once our brief life sets, there is one unending night to be slept through.'[1] Hope was for the living; the dead were without hope.

We must never underestimate the revolutionary distinctiveness of the gospel hope. Those who sleep through Jesus, God will bring with him. That is as certain as the fact that Jesus died and rose again, which is why it balances the sentence. It is the fruit of his passion and victory that death is conquered, its sting is drawn, and on that day of the parousia, death will be swallowed up in victory.

Details of the Lord's coming

The next three verses explain that momentous event in some considerable detail. Verse 15 begins by asserting the Lord's own authority, not only for what follows, but what precedes it: 'For this we say to you by the Lord's own word', referring back to verse 14, as well as forward to 15 and 16. By the 'word of the Lord' Paul could be quoting a statement of Jesus otherwise unknown, or loosely referring to his general teaching. But I think he is most likely claiming direct revelation to him as an apostle. Literally, he is speaking 'in the word of the Lord', by which he means that it is not his private opinion, but the full authority of the Lord Jesus lies behind it. So he wants his readers to be absolutely certain about its truth, and its authenticity.

The substance of verse 15 is that those who are alive on earth at the parousia will not have any sort of advantage over the sleeping ones. Once again, the phraseology has led to a great deal of debate. When he says in verse 15, 'we who are left', does that imply that Paul expected the parousia to be in his lifetime? Liberal critics have not been slow to say that if he was wrong about that, perhaps he was wrong about the whole concept. I think Leon Morris answers this well when he says that we should bear in mind that Paul has a habit of classing himself with those to whom he is writing or we might add, about whom he is writing.[2] Because he was alive at the time, it was only natural to write 'we who are alive'! Because he was looking for the Lord's return, he may well have expected it in his lifetime, but then so should every believer, living each day in the light of the coming.

What verse 15 stresses is the very strong negative of the verb: 'we who are alive will certainly *not* precede those who have fallen asleep'. At root, the verb means to do something before somebody else, so as to have an advantage over them. The idea is graphically illustrated in the man who was at the Pool of Bethesda, who told Jesus, 'While I am trying to get in, someone else goes down ahead of me' (John 5:7). He gets the advantage over me, because he is there first. So, Paul is saying here that to be alive on earth won't give you any advantage at the parousia, except that you won't have to go through death, and we may think that is a considerable advantage! But certainly, in terms of preceding those who have fallen asleep, it will be quite the opposite.

At first sight, this may seem to be labouring a fairly unimportant point. But when we get to verse 16, we realise how its implications are explored more fully. 'For the Lord himself will come down from heaven, with a loud command, with the voice of the archangel and with the trumpet call of God, and the dead in Christ will rise first.' That presents us with a difficulty. How can the Lord bring the dead with him (v. 14) if at the same time as he comes, the dead will rise (v. 16)? The answer is that the parousia is the moment when the spirits of just men made perfect will be united with their resurrection bodies, patterned on the glorious body of the Lord Jesus. It explains why previous generations called the cemetery, the place of sleeping, God's Acre, because there was sown the body which one day will be raised. Paul explains to the Corinthians: 'The body that is sown is perishable, it is raised imperishable; it is sown in dishonour, it is raised in glory; it is sown in weakness, it is raised in power; it is sown a natural body, it is raised a spiritual body' (1 Cor. 15:42). When will that happen? Well, here we are told, when Jesus comes. At death, the soul is separated from the body. We lay to rest the Christian's earthly cottage in the faith that its occupant is with Christ in his immediate presence, which is better by far. And on that day there will be two reunions – the reunion of the redeemed soul with the resurrected body, and the reunion of all the people of God with the Lord and with one another.

The emphasis in verse 16 is all on the Lord's initiative and therefore the inevitability of it all happening. The Lord himself will visibly descend, just as he once visibly ascended – this same Jesus. Every eye will see, every knee will bow. The imagery of verse 16 all works to this end. The word of command is perhaps a reminder that it is the Lord's word alone that can raise the dead. The Lord himself will come down from heaven with a loud command, as Jesus also taught: 'I tell you the truth, a time is coming and has now come when the dead will hear the voice of the Son of God and those who hear will live' (John 5:25). That obviously has a gospel application, and fulfilment, for as the hymn says, 'He speaks, and listening to his voice, new life the dead receive.' But a few verses later in John, we see that there is more to it than that. 'Do not be amazed at this, for a time is coming [it hasn't yet come but it is coming] when all who are in their graves will hear his voice and come out – those who have done good will rise to live, and those who have done evil will rise to be condemned' (John 5:28). So the general resurrection will come about because of the voice of Christ. He raises the dead by his Word. And in 1 Thessalonians the voice of the loud command and of the archangel is matched with the trumpet call of God. We do not have to imagine that they are three separate events, but each of them is a picture of an overwhelming summons that cannot be avoided. The trumpet call, with the involvement of the angels again derives from the teaching of Jesus: 'At that time the sign of the Son of Man will appear in the sky, and all the nations of the earth will mourn. They will see the Son of Man coming on the clouds of the sky, with power and great glory. And he will send his angels with a loud trumpet call, and they will gather his elect from the four winds, from one end of the heavens to the other' (Matt. 24:30-31).

Paul wants his readers to have no doubt about the authority of the Lord who comes. He comes with command, he comes with a trumpet call and the dead are raised. The specific reference here is not to the general resurrection, but that the dead in Christ

will rise first. The order is important. Only after the resurrection
of the dead, in the reunion of souls and risen bodies, will those
who are still alive be caught up together with them to meet the
Lord in the air, changed into his likeness 'in the twinkling of an
eye' (1 Cor. 15:51-52). Paul is underlining that being on earth at
the parousia will not give any advantage. You don't go first!
For the believers living on earth, the parousia will be an
experience of being 'snatched up' (sometimes called the 'rapture'
from the Latin verb meaning 'to seize'). There has been a great
deal of speculation about this event in many Christian circles
during our century. But this verse is the clearest, unambiguous
teaching on the subject in the whole of the New Testament, I
think. The Greek verb *arpaxein* has an element of violence and
suddenness to it. We will be snatched up to meet the Lord in the
air. It is used in John 10:12 of the wolf seizing the sheep, or in
Acts 8:39 of the Spirit snatching Philip away from the Ethiopian
chancellor. Most evocatively, it is used in the Septuagint version
of Genesis 5:24, 'Enoch walked with God. Then he was no more
because God snatched him away.'

What Paul is saying is that the parousia will demonstrate the
irresistible power of the living Lord to reunite all his people in
his presence. No one, believer or unbeliever, can resist it, and
no believer will miss it. That is stressed in the phrase, 'together
with them' (v. 17). So the whole church, united for the first
time, will meet the Lord in the air. He is sovereign in the air, as
he is on earth and in heaven. The clouds, of course, are a picture
of his divine majesty and glory. Elsewhere, Paul calls the devil
'the prince of the power of the air' (Eph. 2:2). But in the place
where Satan has exercised his limited power, Christ and his
glorified people will be united, in celebration of his sovereign
authority and victorious reign.

The comfort to the Thessalonians would be that this great
assurance, which gives them so much hope, cannot be resisted
or hindered by any power, human or demonic. It provides a
fascinating reflection on what Paul said in 2:18. Satan may be
able to hinder Paul from coming to them in the present, but on

the day when the Lord Jesus is revealed in all his glory, nothing will be able to stop the fulfilment of his purposes, and so we shall be with the Lord for ever. It is hard to imagine anything more encouraging or enriching than that knowledge, or anything more calculated to stir our hope and strengthen our perseverance. It isn't even heaven that is our ultimate joy and blessing; it is the Lord himself. Jesus said, 'If I go and prepare a place for you, I will come back and take you to be with me that you also may be where I am' (John 14:3). So we will be with the Lord for ever. It is that certain! 'Therefore encourage each other with these words.' Come alongside and help one another, strengthen one another. Use these words to overcome the sadness and the anxieties about those who have died, because the word of the Lord is to be the means by which grief is turned to consolation and by which fear changes to hope. These are indeed great and wonderful words.

However, our generation is one in which many Christians are largely in ignorance about this great hope of the gospel. There has been comparatively little teaching about the certainties of heaven or the coming of the Lord in recent years, and what there has been has often been eccentric and sometimes fanatical. Many have seen teaching on the second coming as the preserve of cranks and extremists, too difficult and esoteric to understand. But we do ourselves a great disservice if we remain in ignorance both about 'the coming' and about what happens to Christians when they die.

Implications of our Lord's coming

The Thessalonian church needed to know and hold on to these realities, because when the going gets tough, and they were increasingly aware that they were a minority group in a largely hostile environment, then Christians need these certainties to nerve them. This helps to explain why the eschatological material is so important in Paul's second letter to this young church. Its teaching can help us to understand fully the implications of what we have been studying. In 2 Thessalonians 1:3, Paul begins very characteristically: 'We ought always to thank God for you, brothers, and rightly so, because your faith is growing more and more, and the love every one of you has for each other is increasing. Therefore, among God's churches we boast about your perseverance and faith in all the persecutions and trials you are enduring.' So what he has pleaded for in 1 Thessalonians is being fulfilled. Faith is growing and love is increasing in spite of the continuing persecutions and trials. There is perseverance, but Paul wants to motivate that even more, which he does by reintroducing in verse 5 and the following verses the theme of the parousia.

> [5]All this is evidence that God's judgment is right, and as a result you will be counted worthy of the kingdom of God, for which you are suffering. [6]God is just: He will pay back trouble to those who trouble you [7]and give relief to you who are troubled, and to us as well. This will happen when the Lord Jesus is revealed from heaven in blazing fire with his powerful angels. [8]He will punish those who do not know God and do not obey the gospel of our Lord Jesus. [9]They will be punished with everlasting destruction and shut out from the presence of the Lord and from the majesty of his power [10]on the day he comes to be glorified in his holy people and to be marvelled at among all those who have believed. This includes you, because you believed our testimony to you (2 Thess. 1:5-10).

Here, Paul is using the coming of the Lord as both a motivation to persevere and also a comfort in the present suffering. But the emphasis in 2 Thessalonians, in these few verses, is on the other side of the parousia: What will it mean to those who do not know God? The answer is in verse 8: 'He will punish those who do not know God', which is exactly the same phrase that we saw earlier in 1 Thessalonians 4:5: 'passionate lusts like the heathen, who do not know God.' They do not know God so they do not obey the gospel of Christ. Because they do not obey the gospel they cannot come to know God. Clearly, this ignorance and disobedience is culpable, because it brings punishment.

So one of the great impacts that a right view of the parousia makes is that it shapes up the difference between the church and the world so clearly. When we read the opening verses of 2 Thessalonians, we develop a picture of the church as a beleaguered minority group, which is persecuted, undergoing trials (v. 4), suffering and being troubled (v. 6). But the parousia totally reverses that assessment. It is described in verse 7 as a revelation (the Lord Jesus is revealed) in the sense that it shows us what the unseen, hidden reality has always been all the time the church was suffering. When the curtain is pulled back, the Lord Jesus is revealed in blazing fire because he is the ultimate reality. So the parousia is a revelation of God's judgment (v. 5), when his justice will both reward and punish. It is a time of retribution (v. 6) when God will pay back trouble to those who trouble believers. It will mean retribution for the troublers, but relief for the troubled, because the reality that is revealed is that Jesus is Lord. The only way to be ready for that ultimate revelation in blazing fire, of the all-consuming holiness and majesty of God, is to obey the gospel, and through repentance and faith to come to know the living God. For that day will make the distinction between believers and others unmistakably clear and final. The punishment will be exclusion from the presence of the Lord (v. 9). In all his majesty and power he comes and he rejects, he shuts out those who are punished with everlasting destruction. Just as the believer will be with the Lord for ever, so for the unbelieving and the disobedient there will be separation from the Lord's presence for ever. The word translated 'destruction' could be translated 'disaster' or 'ruin'. Clearly the phrase 'everlasting destruction' is the opposite of 'everlasting life'. The punishment is unending separation from the face of the Lord and from the splendour of his majesty.

Everything then will depend on our relationship with him now. That is why verse 10 contrasts the state of the believer with the wicked 'on the day he comes to be glorified in his holy people and to be marvelled at among all those who have believed'. That will be a great day indeed when his people glorify and honour him, and their very existence is a testimony to his glory and honour in the gospel. But the only way to the blessings of that day is to receive the gospel, to obey it as it really is – the word of God – and to live to please God.

To see the end of everything in that perspective helps us to realise why Paul wants the Thessalonians to be joyful and confident in this assurance, which they can have in the face of death and in the light of the return of the Lord Jesus Christ. But it is something we really need to hold on to as well. We need the same distinctiveness to be built into our understanding of our contemporary church situation, because all of these passages are really marking out the distinctiveness of the church from the world. That is the mark of authentic gospel work. In so many ways today, the church resembles, reflects and even mimics the world. We are treated by the world as just another special-interest minority group, and we start to behave that way. They pull the strings and we do the jumping. So our Christianity withdraws from the public arena into a private ghetto, where although exactly the same characteristics of the spirit of the age are revealed, we dress them up in respectable Christian clothes. Is that not why the success-driven ambitionism of the contemporary world is so visible in the church? We play down the end-point and taking on the colour of the world around us, we concentrate on the present. Because our hope doesn't animate us, because we have really lost sight of the day of reckoning, we lose our perseverance, and soon we cave in to the pressures of our culture. We are in the business of accommodation and compromise. We no longer present any provocation to the pagan culture to make us worth the effort of persecuting. We don't speak much about heaven or hell; we are embarrassed by rewards and punishments; we hardly mention eternity, let alone eternal destruction. And so we preach a gospel which is no longer to be obeyed, but to be accepted, and we are not so interested in knowing the true and living God, or even in serving him. Our interest in the contemporary church is often in knowing personal fulfilment, satisfaction, forgiveness, which can so quickly shade over into indulgence, tolerance, understanding, until almost anything goes.

I have talked recently with several Christians who recognize that they have problems in their lives about certain issues which they know to be sin, but whose attitude has become, 'But I know that the Lord understands all about my little faults and he is not going to be too hard on me.' Now, at one level of course, it is true that God is gracious and merciful beyond our imagining. But that sort of self-indulgence can quickly shade into a tolerance of things that do not please God. The woolliness and merging of issues, which can easily result from this, is very characteristic of our contemporary situation. Far from the parousia dominating our horizon, motivating us to holiness, deepening our encourage-ment and stimulating our perseverance, the arrival of the Lord would come to many twentieth century believers as an unwelcome intrusion into the plans they have for building a kingdom of heaven on earth. I think that is why many Christians find death so difficult to cope with. It explains why some have to substitute a Christianised utopia for heaven, as though the real emphasis is getting it all here on earth.

There is a great danger that we lose sight of the coming Lord, and of this glorious fact that we shall be with him for ever. If we do that, we will give up on proclaiming Christ and substitute a desire to fill our churches. Instead of asking that we might be counted worthy of the kingdom of God, we wonder whether the kingdom of God is really worthy of our time and trouble. Does not the contemporary church in the Western world badly need to recover its true perspective of hope before it is too late? We need to build it into our personal lives and we need to re-establish it as a major strand of our ministry. <u>We must reassert the far horizon which makes sense of all that is happening in the present</u>. Almost every New Testament book seems to say that somewhere, and both Thessalonian letters major on the theme, proclaiming it loud and long. It is only the hope of the future that makes sense of what is happening in the present. The way ahead must surely be for us, as it was for Paul, in prayer.

'11With this in mind, we constantly pray for you, that our God may count you worthy of his calling, and that by his power he may fulfil every good purpose of yours and every act prompted by your faith. 12We pray this so that the name of our Lord Jesus may be glorified in you, and you in him, according to the grace of our God and the Lord Jesus Christ' (2 Thess. 1:11-12).

7

A Hope that Endures (2)
1 Thessalonians 5:1-11

[1]Now, brothers, about times and dates we do not need to write to you, [2]for you know very well that the day of the Lord will come like a thief in the night. [3]While people are saying, 'Peace and safety', destruction will come on them suddenly, as labour pains on a pregnant woman, and they will not escape.

[4]But you, brothers, are not in darkness so that this day should surprise you like a thief. [5]You are all sons of the light and sons of the day. We do not belong to the night or to the darkness. [6]So then, let us not be like others, who are asleep, but let us be alert and self-controlled. [7]For those who sleep, sleep at night, and those who get drunk, get drunk at night. [8]But since we belong to the day, let us be self-controlled, putting on faith and love as a breastplate, and the hope of salvation as a helmet. [9]For God did not appoint us to suffer wrath but to receive salvation through our Lord Jesus Christ. [10]He died for us so that, whether we are awake or asleep, we may live together with him. [11]Therefore encourage one another and build each other up, just as in fact you are doing (1 Thessalonians 5:1-11).

The opening of chapter 5 bears a marked similarity to 4:9, where Paul says about brotherly love 'we don't need to write'. Now it is about times and dates that he does not need to write. He is moving on from new teaching about the relationship of Christians who have died to the coming of the Lord Jesus. But he does so by going back, to teach them what they already know, in order to apply it to the current situation in Thessalonica. This is something he has already taught them, so that he did not really need to write further about it. But just as he encourages them to go on in love and faith 'more and more', so his teaching goes back over the basics again and again. Perhaps it is because there is a good deal of excitement and even fanaticism in Thessalonica over the parousia that Paul takes time to remind them of things they should know. It is a wise and proven pastoral method.

Historically, the hope of an imminent coming has always tended to lead to an over-enthusiasm which tries to imagine the event into existence. In our own century, there have been groups of Christians who have been so convinced about the coming of the Lord that they have believed that if only their faith were strong enough, it could produce the actual event. That is usually followed later by disillusionment that the coming seems to have been so long delayed and even loss of faith. In Thessalonica, disputes were developing about its timing, which meant that Paul had to remind them what they had already been told, that no one knows when it will happen. The certainty of the day of the Lord is beyond dispute, but the image of the thief in the night means that it is totally sudden and unexpected.

That idea is further developed in verse 3 where the burglar imagery means that the peace and security the householder imagines himself to be in is actually totally illusory. In fact, sudden disaster and ruin can strike quite unpredictably. A few years ago, on one famous Sunday morning at 4 am, my wife woke me up and said there was a burglar trying to get into the room underneath us. And I said, 'No, don't be silly! It's four o'clock on a Sunday morning; it couldn't possibly be happening.' I turned over to go back to sleep again, but of course she was right and I was wrong. Well, he hadn't sent me a postcard! He hadn't told me he was coming. I didn't really believe he would be there, but there he was, with a crowbar, trying to get into our living room.

Unpredictability – that's the image of the thief. On the other hand, the image of the pregnant woman teaches inevitability. Now these are things that Christians know – the coming of the Lord is going to happen inevitably, just as labour pains inevitably tell about the birth that is going to come. But there is also an unpredictability about it – the world does not even know that this event is going to happen. And once again, Paul is drawing a line of distinction between the brothers and the others. He is giving them further assurance that they really have got the right message and that they are on track. This is further evidence of what it means to belong to the brothers, and it automatically separates you from the others. The Thessalonians have probably requested some sort of information about the timing. It may be that they asked him for something clear and accurate and he answers them by saying that all they can know 'accurately' (v. 2) is that they cannot know when he is going to come. So his ironic answer is that you can know as accurately as you can predict a thief's arrival, when the day of the Lord will be. But the certainty of the event is one hundred percent assured.

The Old Testament background to the 'day of the Lord', which is the biblical context in mind here, is usually judgment against his enemies. But that very judgment spells salvation for God's people through the destruction of those who oppose them. It is important in this passage to keep in mind that the Lord's visitation is always double-edged in Scripture. When God visited his people Israel in Egypt, it was to bring wrath on Pharaoh in the plagues, but to rescue his people through the Passover. When he visited his people in Babylon to bring them back from exile, what spelt restoration for the Jews was at the price of Babylon's downfall and capitulation to the Persians. So the day of the Lord in Scripture is always a day both of salvation and of judgment.

At this point, an excursion into 2 Thessalonians 2, which

was probably written a very short time after the first letter, will considerably deepen our understanding.

> ¹Concerning the coming of our Lord Jesus Christ and our being gathered to him, we ask you, brothers, ²not to become easily unsettled or alarmed by some prophecy, report or letter supposed to have come from us, saying that the day of the Lord has already come. ³Don't let anyone deceive you in any way, for that day will not come, until the rebellion occurs and the man of lawlessness is revealed, the man doomed to destruction. ⁴He will oppose and will exalt himself over everything that is called God or is worshipped, so that he sets himself up in God's temple, proclaiming himself to be God.
>
> ⁵Don't you remember that when I was with you I used to tell you these things? ⁶And now you know what is holding him back, so that he may be revealed at the proper time. ⁷For the secret power of lawlessness is already at work; but the one who now holds it back will continue to do so till he is taken out of the way. ⁸And then the lawless one will be revealed, whom the Lord Jesus will overthrow with the breath of his mouth and destroy by the splendour of his coming. ⁹The coming of the lawless one will be in accordance with the work of Satan displayed in all kinds of counterfeit miracles, signs and wonders, ¹⁰and in every sort of evil that deceives those who are perishing. They perish because they refused to love the truth and so be saved. ¹¹For this reason God sends them a powerful delusion so that they will believe the lie ¹²and so that all will be condemned who have not believed the truth but have delighted in wickedness (2 Thess. 2:1-12).

Here we have an indication that the confusion concerning the events which Paul described in the first letter – the coming of the Lord with his holy ones – was still rampant (vv. 1-2). Their great fear must have been that 'the coming' had already occurred, and some of the Thessalonian Christians had missed it. In fact all of them would have, apart from those who had died! Given our understanding of the teaching in 1 Thessalonians elsewhere, it is very difficult for us to see how anyone could imagine such a climactic event occurring without everyone be-

ing aware of it. On these grounds, some commentators suggest
that the verb should be translated that the coming of the Lord
and our gathering together is about to take place – we don't
want you to be unsettled by reports that it is about to happen.
But it is clearly a past tense at the end of verse 2 – the day of the
Lord has already come – and it is very difficult to see how Paul
could possibly be referring to something that is future. Moreover, Paul's line of thought in verse 3ff. does not deal with that
argument at all. It deals with the supposition that it has already
happened.

There are various other suggestions to solve the problem.
Some indicate that an over-realised eschatology has taken hold
and that the parousia is not so much an external event as an
inward appreciation of the coming of the Spirit in the personal
life of the believer.

But perhaps the most likely solution is that proposed by Ernest
Best in his commentary, which is that the terminology of verse
2 could refer to a complex of events, of which the parousia is
seen as the climax.[1] This would take the 'day of the Lord' to
mean a period of time, which it can mean in the Old Testament,
as well as a literal period of twenty-four hours. On this reading,
what is being said is that the process which will climax in the
parousia, is already under way. If that is the predominant idea in
Thessalonica, then the hyper-enthusiasm, and fanaticism even,
about an imminent coming is much more understandable. There
is an element of biblical sanity in this, in that the period between
the ascension of Christ and the coming is often referred to as
'the last days'. The life of the world to come has already broken
in to this world of time and space, so that in one sense the
eschatological age is already under way. Further light is shed on
the issue from Mark 13, where the Lord Jesus teaches about the
coming: 'Many will come in my name, claiming, "I am he", and
will deceive many' (Mark 13:6). Paul reminds his readers that
there will be deception regarding the coming of the Lord. Some
will come in his name, using prophetic messages or reports, or
perhaps even a letter supposed to have come from an apostle, to

support their thesis. We are not told in 2 Thessalonians that there is an individual who is actually claiming to be the returned Lord Jesus, but we can see in Mark 13 how Jesus deals with that situation, to warn against false excitement about the coming. 'When you hear of wars and rumours of wars, do not be alarmed. Such things must happen, but the end is still to come' (Mark 13:7). And again, a little later, 'When you see "the abomination that causes desolation" standing where it does not belong – let the reader understand – then let those who are in Judea flee to the mountains' (Mark 13:14). So when Jesus is dealing with false expectations about the coming, he has this framework: not yet ... until. Not yet – when you hear of wars and rumours of war; Until – you see the sign of the abomination that causes desolation. Returning to 2 Thessalonians 2, we find the same pattern is there. Are we facing the imminent coming? Paul answers it by saying, 'Not until' – 'Don't let anyone deceive you ... that day will not come, until the rebellion occurs' (v. 3). And again, in verse 7, 'the secret power of lawlessness is already at work' so in that sense we are in the last days, but the one who holds him back will continue to do so, *until* he is taken out of the way. So it does seem that, following our Lord's teaching, Paul expects distinctive signs which will precede the event itself, and which can therefore be identified. This means that deception becomes a very real possibility. The danger is not misunderstanding, so much as being misled by false claims and false prophets, whose deliberate intention is to deceive. Just as Jesus warned, there will be deceivers who will try to fool even the elect about this climactic event, so Paul is not surprised to find deception at work in the church.

The thrust of Paul's response is that certain events must precede the parousia. This means that a time has been fixed in the counsel of God, and a programme has to be worked through, of which verse 3 states the two major ingredients. 'Don't let anyone deceive you in any way, for that day will not come until' – the apostasy occurs and the man of lawlessness is revealed. These are strange and difficult concepts to us, and we may feel that

verse 3 conceals as much as it reveals, but we have to remember
that Paul had instructed the young church about these things
while he was with them. He says in verse 5: 'Don't you remember that when I was with you I used to tell you these things?' So
they knew what he meant, even if we find it hard to reconstruct.

The event that is called 'the rebellion', or the apostasy
(apostasia), is of course a falling-away. The term is widely used
about attempts of the oppressors of the Jews to make them fall
away from the Lord and turn their backs on their Jewish herit-
age and tradition, through the many centuries when the occupy-
ing forces of the land constantly tried to hellenise the Jews. Those
Jews who adopted Greek customs apostasised; they fell away,
they rebelled against the authority of Yahweh. That is the most
common use of the word, and the sense in which Paul is using
it. It seems that the rebellion, the falling-away, that will happen,
is directly related to the other factor, the man of lawlessness
(anomia), who will appear.

The man of lawlessness

The vocabulary concerning this individual is both interesting
and instructive. His appearance is described in eschatological
terminology. It is all apocalyptic. He is to be 'revealed' (v. 3).
That is the same root *(apokalypsis)* as is used of the Lord Jesus
in 2 Thessalonians 1:7, 'when the Lord Jesus is revealed from
heaven in blazing fire'. So the man of lawlessness will be 'revealed' and the point is repeated in verses 6 and 8: 'Now you
know what is holding him back, so that he may be *revealed* at
the proper time', and, 'then the lawless one will be *revealed*'.
And not only will there be an 'apokalypsis' of the lawless one,
but there will be a 'parousia' (v. 9). That vocabulary is clearly
chosen very purposefully. This person's manifestation is Satan's deceptive parody of Jesus' coming. In that sense it is an
anti-parousia of the future coming of the Lord Jesus.

What, then, is this man of lawlessness going to do? Verse 4
tells us that he will oppose and exalt himself over everything
that is called God or worshipped, so that he sets himself up in

God's temple, proclaiming himself to be God. He arrogates to himself the divine attribute of sitting in the temple, and he proclaims his own divinity. That is a theme which takes us straight back to the 'abomination of desolation' in Daniel that is quoted by Jesus in Mark 13. The original historical reference in Daniel was undoubtedly to Antiochus Epiphanes, who in the year 167 BC installed the cult of Zeus in the temple of Jerusalem. What Paul predicts is not without historical precedence. It is the scale and timing of the man of lawlessness that is going to be particularly significant.

The same idea is present in other Old Testament passages. For example, Isaiah 14:12-14, where addressing the king of Babylon, who is portrayed as aspiring to ascend to the throne of heaven, the word of the Lord comes:

> [12]How you have fallen from heaven,
>   O morning star, son of the dawn!
> You have been cast down to the earth,
>   you who once laid low the nations!
> [13]You said in your heart,
>   'I will ascend to heaven;
> I will raise my throne
>   above the stars of God;
> I will sit enthroned on the mount of assembly,
>   on the utmost heights of the sacred mountain.
> [14]I will ascend above the tops of the clouds;
>   I will make myself like the Most High.'

This is a strong likelihood that this taunt song is being sung not only against the king of Babylon, but against the son of the morning, the son of the dawn, Lucifer, and that behind this earthly monarch's attempts to assume divine authority lies the devil's own implacable hostility towards God and man, and his ejection from heaven. But whether we believe that is so or not, very clearly powerful human beings have often arrogated to themselves the position of God. There is a history of it down through the centuries. 'Say to the ruler of Tyre, "This is what the Sover-

eign LORD says: 'In the pride of your heart you say, "I am a god;
I sit on the throne of a god in the heart of the seas"' (Ezek. 28:2).

In the first century, Herod Agrippa receiving divine honours
from the populace of Caesarea is another example (Acts 12:21-
23). In AD 40 the Roman emperor Caligula attempted to have
his statues put up in the temple at Jerusalem to assert his claims
to divinity. This whole idea was not a million miles away from
a first century congregation formed of Jews and God-fearing
Greeks.

What all this points to is a climactic revelation where a su-
preme agent of Satan will be revealed. In his person, all the
hostility of proud humanity to God comes, as it were, to a definitive eschatological head. This person, an incarnation of evil,
parallels the federal headship of fallen humanity in Adam, and
parodies Christ as the head of the new humanity. The man of
lawlessness is a great imitator of Christ, but in a context of utter
evil and total opposition to him. 'The coming of the lawless one
will be in accordance with the work of Satan' just as the coming
of Jesus will be in accordance with the work of God, but here
displayed in all kinds of counterfeit miracles, signs and wonders and in every sort of evil that deceives those who are perishing (2:9).

What Paul is pointing out here is that everything the Lord
Jesus does, and will do, is mimicked by the man of lawlessness.
He will have his own parousia, his own signs and wonders, all
sorts of highly impressive miracles, which will delude and deceive, as the Lord Jesus himself warned us. 'For false Christs
and false prophets will appear and perform great signs and miracles to deceive even the elect, if that were possible. See I have
told you ahead of time' (Matt. 24:24). Those events, occurring
throughout the history of the church, find their fullest focus in
this climactic event immediately before the end. But the mark
of the elect is that they are not deceived. It is those that are
perishing who are the gullible victims. Every sort of evil deceives those who are perishing, because they have refused to
love the truth and so be saved.

So what is happening immediately before the parousia is that people have chosen not to believe the truth, which is the only way of salvation. When you don't believe the truth, then you don't believe nothing, you believe anything, and what verse 11 describes is the lie which they believe. 'For this reason God sends them a powerful delusion so that they will believe the lie.' There is a chilling logical progression here. Falling away is produced by the man of sin who induces unbelievers to accept the lie that he is God. It is all a powerful delusion which God not only permits, but directly visits on those who have delighted in wickedness and refused to believe the truth. For this reason God sends them a powerful delusion so that they will believe the lie and be condemned.

God's judgment is at work in the whole process of the last of the last days, preceding the salvation, as these ultimate rebellions against him are revealed. But without the Christ, the antichrist would be unthinkable. His very existence and rebellion is in itself proof of the reality of Christ and his kingdom. All the deception, all the lies, are only there because his raison-d'être is to fight against everything Christ means in the world. In that sense he is a representative Satanic figure.

It is hardly surprising that from Paul's day onwards, the church has never been short of speculators offering to identify this figure. For, of course, even though we are told that we can't know when the Lord is coming, we imagine that if we could identify the man of lawlessness, we would know! So in the early days it was the Imperial persecutor, either in the person of the Roman state machine, or incarnated in a particular emperor – Septimus Severus was the man of lawlessness; Julian the Apostate in a later century another. Around 180, Irenaeus decided that the focus was on the Jews, responding of course to the pressure in his own generation, and decreed that the man of lawlessness would be a Jew. A Latin commentator of the third century, suggested that the man of lawlessness would be Nero come back to life as a Jew! That way you can have both qualifications, and his new name will add up to – 666!

After Constantine, almost any enemy of Christendom has been a candidate, and you can trace them through history. Mohammed, in the seventh century, was the man of lawlessness. Individual popes and the papacy itself also featured, as in the 1646 *Westminster Confession of Faith* which says the pope of Rome is that man of sin and perdition that exalts himself within the church against Christ and all that is called God. Luther named the pope, and the pope returned the compliment! The pope's men worked out that Luther's name could also be made to add up to 666!

The restrainer

Back in the text, the other vital point to note is verse 7: 'For the secret power of lawlessness is already at work.' Though the individual has yet to be revealed, the reason that has not yet happened is given in verses 6 and 7: 'And now you know what is holding him back, so that he may be revealed at the proper time. For the secret power of lawlessness is already at work; but the one who now holds it back will continue to do so till he is taken out of the way.' Who is this restrainer? In verse 6, the term is neuter – *what* is holding him back. In verse 7, it is masculine – *the one* who holds him back. That is important both to Paul's argument and also to calming the Thessalonian church in its hype about times and dates. It is important that we get this as clear as we can, because their danger is, in fact, our danger, namely that we will be sidetracked from the real purpose of the parousia, and our expectation of it, into extravagant speculation. He had already prepared the church for the man of *anomia*, but there is a power or a person who prevents him from appearing.

Again, there are many suggestions as to what this may be. The most common one is that it was the Roman imperium, the emperor himself, perhaps, or the Roman state, but Leon Morris puts it with his customary clarity when he says, 'If this was Paul's view he was in error, because the Roman empire has passed away and the man of lawlessness has not yet made his appearance.'[2] I think it is a better solution to recognise the verb that is translated as 'holding him back' – '*katakein*'. When it is used intransitively, as it is here, without an object, it often means to hold sway or rule, or to prevail. If you prevail over something, you hold it back. If there is no object that you are prevailing over, then 'holding sway' or 'ruling' is what the verb means. So verse 6 could mean that there is a principle that is holding sway at the moment and which will yield at the proper time to the man of lawlessness being revealed. What is holding sway or prevailing now, in verse 6, is in contrast to the 'then' of verse 8 – 'then the lawless one will be revealed.'

But what is holding sway now, in terms of verse 7, is the secret power of lawlessness, that is the great anti-christian force at work in the world, which we now can see throughout the last twenty centuries in human history. This makes sense of the link word 'for' at the beginning of verse 7. There is a principle that is currently holding sway because the secret power of lawlessness is already at work. But we know that this power can only prevail according to the sovereign will of God. The whole context of 2 Thessalonians 2 shows us that God's timing is the predominant factor. He is the one who is in control of the proper time (v. 6) and he is the one who sends the powerful delusion of the lie (v. 11). So, he is the one who now prevails, even though he allows the forces of evil a great deal of rope. The power of lawlessness already seems to exercise authority, but only under the over-all sovereign will and purpose of God. If God steps aside and allows that force of evil to be focused in this apocalyptic figure, the man of lawlessness, then that will still be under God's sovereign will and timing, and only as the prelude to the coming of the Lord Jesus. All the forces of evil are subject to his total authority at every stage of the process.

The overthrow of the man of lawlessness
Is not verse 8 then magnificent? 'The lawless one will be revealed, whom the Lord Jesus will overthrow with the breath of his mouth and destroy by the splendour of his coming.' It is a great thought that the very breath of the glorified Lord Jesus

will slay the lawless one, like a blast from a fiery furnace. The splendour of his coming is all that is needed. 'He utters his voice; the earth melts' (Ps. 46:6). The 'breath of his mouth' is familiar biblical language for uttering the word of the Lord, which expresses the will of the Lord. All that the Lord Jesus will need to do is to utter his word. He will overthrow him with the breath of his mouth and destroy him by the very splendour of his coming. Just as everything began that way – God said, 'Let there be' and there was – so everything will end that way. He speaks his word and his will is done.

How much we need to develop that confidence in the power of the word of the Lord Jesus for ourselves today! Our problem is that we tend to think that God's words are like our words. Our words are carried on our breath, just as God's word is carried by his breath, his Spirit. But while our words express our thoughts, they do not execute our will. The difference is that when God speaks, it is done. His word is sufficient. So the breath of the Lord, who is the living Word, will destroy and bring to nothing the most powerful demonstration of anti-God forces the world has ever seen. There isn't even a contest. The Lord Jesus will overthrow him with the breath of his mouth.

The certainty of the parousia
We now return to 1 Thessalonians and our original passage in chapter 5. Perhaps now we can see what strength and encouragement these two passages breathe into the Thessalonian church and into ourselves. Here is the renewal of our hope. What Paul is teaching us is that nothing is going to prevent the parousia of the Lord Jesus and the total victory which it will represent. It is urgent that we should not succumb to fanciful speculations which have no credentials. The Thessalonians are to hold on to the apostolic teaching validated in Paul's original ministry of the gospel among them. The same is true for us today. Like them, we have believed the truth. We do have the faith that works, so we are not going to be deluded by the lie. We are being sanctified through the Spirit and we will share in the glory of the Lord

Jesus. That is why we are 'not in darkness so that this day should
surprise you like a thief' (5:4). There is something that Christians know that others do not know, and as a result there is a
way that Christians live which others cannot live. That's the
great distinctive, the dividing line. That is what marks the brothers out from the others. Once again, Paul is combining belief
and behaviour. The proof of the faith that works is in terms of
the labouring love and the hope that perseveres. The way we
live is the evidence of the reality of what we believe. So, our
distinctive beliefs about the end produce a distinctive lifestyle
in the present. This means that the day of the Lord will not surprise us like a thief. We are prepared. Best makes the point well
in his commentary when he says, 'Only the unprepared are surprised by the unexpected.'[3]

Contrasting lifestyles

In verses 4-7, the contrast of lifestyles is expressed in four sets
of opposites – day and night, light and darkness, alert and asleep,
sober and drunk. If we are in the dark about spiritual realities,
then the Lord's parousia will be like the thief in the night. But
the Christian is not in the dark. Those who trust in Christ have
been illumined by the Light of the World. Darkness is a biblical
picture of ignorance, sometimes of separation. That is why the
verb in verse 4 is slightly hostile and threatening. It is the idea
of being overtaken. 'Surprise' in the NIV is a neutral word, but
the original idea is that this day should not 'overtake' us like a
thief. By contrast, all Christians are sons of the light and sons of
the day (v. 5). The Lord Jesus spoke about the people of this
world and the children of light, and taught his disciples: 'Put
your trust in the light while you have it, so that you may become
sons of the light' (John 12:36). So those who trust in Christ are
sons of the light. They are sons of the day, which in this context
has the added reference to waiting expectantly for Jesus to come.

On the basis of what has already happened and who we already are, then come the practical applications of verse 6. 'We
do not belong to the night or to the darkness. So then, let us' –

and there are three exhortations which contrast Christians with the others.

'Let us not be like others, who are asleep', is the first one. Let us not sleep like the householder who has no idea of the imminence of the burglar. Others may be unconscious of the Lord's coming, but we cannot behave like them. Secondly, let us be 'alert', or awake. And thirdly, let us be 'self-controlled', sober, clear-headed. Those two practical attitudes contrast strongly with the sleep and drunkenness which are characteristic of what goes on at night. But more concretely, Paul is saying that waiting for Jesus means living disciplined lives. It means actively expecting his return, not getting sidetracked into endless discussions about the identity of the man of lawlessness and whether he has appeared, but wanting to be found faithful to our Lord and King, so that we get on with the business of a faith that works, a love that labours and a hope that perseveres. Then, at his coming, we shall not be ashamed, not caught out. That is how we demonstrate that we have a real hope in his coming and that we live these days in the light of that day.

Several years ago was the centenary year of my daughter's school, during which they were honoured with a visit from the Queen. The amount of work which went on to prepare for the royal visit was phenomenal. Parts of the school that had not seen paint for years and years suddenly appeared pristine, bright and shining. The whole school site was tidied up and everything possible was done, so that it was absolutely ready for the great day. Can you imagine the chaos and embarrassment if a royal visit were to be announced, but nobody really believed it was going to happen, so nobody bothered to get ready! But isn't that exactly what is going to happen when the King comes?

It is totally uncharacteristic of people who acknowledge the Lordship of Jesus, for him to come as their King from heaven and find them completely unready. How can they claim to be his citizens? How can they claim to believe his Word? It is a matter of complete contradiction. That is why we are to take seriously the exhortations to be alert and self-controlled. And that is why we need to show we believe in the second coming by working out the practical implications of verse 8: 'Putting on faith and love as a breastplate and the hope of salvation as a helmet.' You see, it would be no good going around Thessalonica proclaiming that their King is coming if the lives that they were living denied their assertion. It is no good having endless advent testimony meetings if we are not living holy lives. This verse explains what being sober and self-controlled actually means. It means faith, love and hope. It is exactly what we saw right at the beginning of the letter: 'your faith that works, your love that labours, your hope that perseveres' (1:3).

It is very probable that Paul is using Isaiah's picture of Jesus the Messiah as the anointed conqueror coming to rescue his people. Bible translations often give a cross-reference to Isaiah 59:17, which is a picture of the King coming to save. 'He put on righteousness as his breastplate, and the helmet of salvation on his head'; and in the preceding verse, 'his own arm worked salvation for him, and his own righteousness sustained him.' To be ready for the King then, is to follow in his footsteps.

An achieved salvation
Before we leave verse 8, there is a further important little point to note. The NIV translation uses a present participle: 'since we belong to the day, let us be self-controlled, putting on...' The implication of that is, first of all I am self-controlled, and because I am self-controlled, then I can put on faith, hope and love. But actually the original is a past participle. 'Since we belong to the day, let us be self-controlled, having put on faith and love as a breastplate and the hope of salvation as a helmet.' Doesn't that make a great deal more sense? The NIV implies that this is something that we do, because we *are* self-controlled, whereas the past participle explains how we can be self-controlled. After all, a soldier puts on the equipment before he goes out on guard-duty so that he is able to do the job. Similarly, if believers are going to be ready for the day of the Lord, and properly equipped when the King comes, then the breast-

plate and helmet that we wear have got to be put on first. They
have been put on when we became Christians, and we have got
to keep ourselves fully armed 'more and more'. We are already
wearing that breastplate; we do trust him, we do love him. We
already have the helmet of the hope of our salvation. We are
waiting for Jesus who will rescue us from the coming wrath.
That is how we keep ourselves ready. And although that salvation is already being experienced in a measure, obviously the
focus is strongly eschatological. We will experience salvation
in its fulness on that day when he comes to bring in the fulness
of his kingdom.

This knowledge is a great motivator towards consistent Christian living. 'For God did not appoint us to suffer wrath but to
receive salvation through our Lord Jesus Christ' (v. 9). That is
why we have to be watchful and self-controlled, and it is why
he has given us the armour of faith and love and hope. We now
know what lies at the end of the road. We know that the road
divides into wrath and salvation, but it is not that Christians
now are working hard in order to secure their salvation, as though
their sanctification were the ground of their justification. Far
from it! The argument in verse 9 is that it is God's appointment
that we will receive salvation. That was why Paul gave thanks
in chapter 1 for their faith and love and hope, and saw it as the
sign that God has chosen them. Here the two thoughts are linked
together again. A mark of God having chosen you, the fact that
you can have assurance that you will receive salvation, that you
are appointed to that at the last day, is that now you are exhibit-
ing faith, love and hope. Do so, 'more and more'.

No longer in a position of condemnation, which would make
us suffer wrath, God has literally put us in this particular position of salvation. He has appointed us to receive it, and all because our Lord Jesus Christ 'died for us so that, whether we are
awake or asleep, we may live together with him' (v. 10). Our
hope of salvation, then, will prove to be a reality, because the
coming King and Judge is also the Rescuer. He is the one who
died for us. Our future hope is securely grounded in the past at

the Cross of Calvary, and so must our present Christian living be. We believe that Jesus died and rose again; so we believe that God will bring with Jesus those who have fallen asleep (4:14). 'He died for us so that, whether we are awake or asleep, we may live together with him' (5:10). Therefore, we live together with him now in the knowledge that we shall be together with him for ever. The exalted Lord who achieves this salvation is the crucified Jesus; he died for us, in our place, on our behalf. And the purpose of that great salvation is not just to rescue us from wrath, wonderful though that is, beyond our present understanding, but it is also that we will live together with him. 'We will be with the Lord for ever. Therefore encourage each another with these words' (4:17-18).

Encourage one another

Verse 10 picks up that metaphor of being awake or asleep, not now talking about spiritually being alive or dead to God, but going back to its original use when he talked about Christians who died as 'falling asleep'. We might paraphrase the verse, 'He died for us so that whether we are alive in the body on earth, or whether we have gone on into his presence in heaven, we may live together with him.' That is the purpose of his death on the cross, and just as death has been overcome through the death of Jesus, so we shall share that victory.

We have come full circle now from 4:14. It is really one long unit from 4:14 to 5:11, and we have come back now to this whole business of whether we are alive when the Lord comes, or whether we have died, with the certain knowledge that either way we will be living with him for ever. Everything is grounded in the work of Christ for us, and our union with him accomplished through faith. So when we recognise how far reaching that change is and how certain of it we can be, then we must live godly lives of faith, love and hope, because we have to live today in the light of eternity. That is the great source of encouragement and strengthening to which verse 11 refers: 'Encourage one another and build each other up.' The encouragement comes through building one another up in our conviction concerning the reality of these things. This idea is often developed in Paul's later letters. We cannot build ourselves up in isolation. We build one another up in love. That is both how faith works and how love labours.

We do need to restore this corporate responsibility of fellowship as a priority in our churches. It is fine to have a cup of something after the service for people to chat, but it is important that we understand how to use those precious few minutes to maximum effect, to strengthen one another. People lead such busy lives these days, and fellowship is almost a luxury, but times like that can have tremendous impact. We don't want to make people artificial about it or to think they have to talk piously all the time, but we do need to use our times of fellowship so that they are strengthening and building up the church. So often it is a catalogue of moans and groans of all that has gone wrong in the week, which prompts the hearer to get away as quickly as possible and talk to somebody else! Whereas the sort of love that says 'Well, let's sit down and talk for a while and pray about things' is such a refreshment. Such a conversation can focus on the wonderful hope we have of the Lord's return. I don't mean that in a glib way but simply to rejoice that we do know the end of the story and we do have a sure and certain hope. You see, a church where that sort of thing is happening naturally is a church that is distinguished from the others. There is no excuse in the future hope for being idle and not caring. There is every incentive and every encouragement to love and to labour. And there is plenty of work to be done in the congregation.

Verse 11 says, 'just as in fact you are doing', but brothers, I want you to do it 'more and more'. The flagship church always needs to keep teaching and encouraging these great basics of the faith. If your faith in God is known everywhere, all over Greece, and all over Asia Minor, as they all tell how you have turned to God (1:8-9), then it is very important that you keep on encouraging one another and building each other up, so that people can see this gospel is not just a flash in the pan but a consistency of lifestyle. We must never get to the stage where we think we have progressed beyond these things. That sort of progress is totally illusory, isn't it? It may appeal to our human pride but it actually moves us away from the reality of serving and waiting.

Paul is clearly digging in for a long wait. His teaching about the parousia combines the two ingredients that we find so hard to hold together. He stresses the imminence of the coming, but he does not assert its immediacy. He is preparing them for a long haul. If the immediacy were the important ingredient, as the extreme group in Thessalonica seems to have believed, then the timing would presumably be known, which Paul rejects as a possibility, since there would not then be any intervening course of events such as 2 Thessalonians 2 has described. Rather, it is the imminence of the coming that actually gets us on track. Obviously in a situation of stress and persecution, the hope of the coming will be an enormous strengthener to faith, but its non-happening, if you think it is going to happen tomorrow, will be an equal discouragement on the day after tomorrow. Paul is looking for a consistency of hope. He is counteracting the roller-coaster effect that is taking over in Thessalonica. He concentrates on the cultivation of normal Christian character – daily, disciplined obedience. That is the mark of reality which he already sees in the church and which he wants to go on cultivating 'more and more'. That hope, rightly understood, has an ethical and moral imperative – Let us be alert and self-controlled, having put on faith, love and hope, for God did not appoint us to suffer wrath, but to receive salvation.

And although we are so much nearer to the great event than Paul was, we certainly need that same encouragement to establish those same priorities for ourselves.

8

A God Who Will Do It
1 Thessalonians 5:12-28

[12]Now we ask you, brothers, to respect those who work hard among you, who are over you in the Lord and who admonish you. [13]Hold them in the highest regard in love because of their work. Live in peace with each other. [14]And we urge you, brothers, warn those who are idle, encourage the timid, help the weak, be patient with everyone. [15]Make sure that nobody pays back wrong for wrong, but always try to be kind to each other and to everyone else.

[16]Be joyful always; [17]pray continually; [18]give thanks in all circumstances, for this is God's will for you in Christ Jesus.

[19]Do not put out the Spirit's fire; [20]do not treat prophecies with contempt. [21]Test everything. Hold on to the good. [22]Avoid every kind of evil.

[23]May God himself, the God of peace, sanctify you through and through. May your whole spirit, soul and body be kept blameless at the coming of our Lord Jesus Christ. [24]The one who calls you is faithful and he will do it.

[25]Brothers, pray for us. [26]Greet all the brothers with a holy kiss. [27]I charge you before the Lord to have this letter read to all the brothers.

[28]The grace of our Lord Jesus Christ be with you (1 Thess. 5:12-28).

On reading this passage, one can feel some sympathy with the NIV translators when they throw in the towel with a catch-all heading like 'Final Instructions', which says everything and nothing. However, we do know from experience that Paul does not let his letters dribble on to an anticlimactic end, but that they are always shaped towards a powerful conclusion, and certainly verses 23 and 24 provide that here.

We have just been reminded in 5:11 that this is a letter of encouragement, and it will not do us any harm to replay the reasons for this. Here is a church which we have recognized has become a flagship church. It is a church that is widely known for its faith, love and hope. These Thessalonian Christians are on track. They have got the real gospel. They have been ministered to by a real apostle. They have believed the truth and that truth is experientially at work in their lives. But the characteristic of being on track is that faith, love and hope are developed more and more. So, Paul gives himself to addressing what he describes as 'what is lacking in your faith' (3:10). They lack understanding of the effect that the parousia will have on those who have died in Christ. They lack understanding about how to deal with the excitement that is around in Thessalonica about the times and seasons regarding the Lord's coming. Some of them have lacked understanding about the godly lives they should be living, the holiness that should be characteristic of them. Some others, it seems, are in danger of destroying the love that exists between them by not caring how their behaviour affects others. There is much to encourage in Thessalonica, and to be encouraged about, but there is also a good deal more to be done to build on this promising start.

In this final section, then, we shall not be surprised to find a number of these issues re-surfacing. It will be helpful firstly to see the structure on which it is built, which is, in fact, a series of triplets. Verses 12 and 13 deal with relationships with the leaders of the church. They have three tasks and there are three responses to them. Verse 14 identifies three areas of particular need in the church, each of which has a remedy that is outlined. The idle have to be warned, the timid encouraged, the weak helped.

Verses 14b to 15 define three general duties or expressions of Christian love that labours. It must be patient, not revengeful and kind.

Verses 16 and 17 outline three characteristics of God's will in the believer's life – joy, prayer, thanksgiving.

Verses 19 to 22 deal with the area of spiritual gifts, ending with three positives: test, hold on to the good, avoid the evil.

In fact, this triplet motif seems to extend even into verse 24, where Paul prays for the spirit, soul and body to be kept blameless at the coming of the Lord Jesus. Those who are preachers of sermons will be thrilled to know that the 'three pointer' has been with us from the very beginning!

Leadership

We will consider firstly the area of relationships with the leaders covered in verses 12-13. Before we come to the attitude that Paul wants to inculcate within the church, we need to concentrate on the qualities of leadership which he looks for and, indeed, commands. It is very unlikely that Paul had appointed these leaders, since he had only been in the city for three Sabbath days, it seems. Some, who were converts from the synagogue, may perhaps have been rulers of the synagogue already: they may have taken over ruling positions in the church, but the important issue is to understand how Christian leadership is to be recognised and approved. I rather like the observation that a leader is a person whom other people follow. If you are out in front and no one else is following, you are not a leader, you are just going for a walk! So, here are three characteristics of real Christian leaders, Paul says. They work hard among you, they are over you in the Lord, and they admonish you (v. 12).

Why is it important for the Thessalonians, and for us, to understand this? Leaders must *work hard*. The word describes physical labour, hard, backbreaking toil, which Paul often uses about spiritual work in his letters. We have had it before in verb form in verse 3 of chapter 1 – 'your labour prompted by love', or in the original, your love that labours – so the fruit of love is this sort of hard work. Real leaders, then, work hard out of love. In 2:9 it was used about Paul's commitment, his toil and hardship by which he worked night and day in order not to be a burden to any of them while he preached the gospel. And in 3:5, he uses it to refer to his ministry in Thessalonica, 'our efforts' the NIV translates it, or, literally, our hard work, our labours. 'We did not want our labours to prove to be useless.' It is very characteristic of Paul and very much a characteristic of true Christian leaders that they toil to meet the needs of the church.

We all know what hard work Christian leadership is, but the more you are committed to it, of course, in a sense the less people notice it, and that must be a good thing. Paul is not advocating a self-conscious attitude of 'Do you know how hard I work?' Rather, this is a love that will not let other people go, that insists on working for their best in every situation. The true leader is not obsessed about proving how hard he is working, which is actually a worldly way of looking at things. His attention is far too much on the flock and their benefit to be diverted by that kind of introspection, which is what makes him an effective leader.

Secondly, leaders are 'over you in the Lord'. This is quite a difficult concept to translate, because again it is one of those verbs that has a wide range of meaning, and it is worthwhile seeing its range in other parts of the New Testament. In 1 Timothy 5:17, Paul uses this verb when he says, 'The elders who direct the affairs of the church well are worthy of double honour.' That is the first meaning of the verb – to direct, to rule, which the NIV picks up here by its translation 'over you in the Lord'. But it has an equally widely used meaning, a derivative from that, which is 'being concerned about' and 'caring for'. The idea within the verb is not a dictatorial oversight, but a pastoral care and concern. The leader is one whose love for the flock prompts him to work hard and enables him to care for them.

The root meaning of the verb is 'stand before', which can be understood as the role of a protector who stands between the sheep and the wolf. Paul uses it in that sense in Titus 3:8: 'I want you to stress these things, so that those who have trusted in God may be careful to devote themselves to doing what is good.' That 'careful devotion' is this verb, meaning that they may be concerned, may take care over, devoting themselves to what is good. It comes again in Titus 3:14: 'Our people must learn to take care over doing what is good in order to provide for daily necessities.'

The two ideas come together in 1 Timothy 3:4, where Paul talks about the overseer or church leader managing his own family well. If he does not know how to manage his own family, that is both how to be the head of it and also to take care of it, how can he take care of God's church (3:5)? It is repeated in 3:12: 'A deacon must be the husband of but one wife and must manage his children and his household well.' That provides us with a basic understanding of the way in which Paul uses this verb. The leader is 'over you in the Lord', but he is over you as a father is over his household, caring for, managing it, concerned about it, seeking at all times to protect it. The nature of Christian leadership is hard work, combined with that sort of care.

Lastly, the leader's task is to admonish. This verb (*noutheteo*) presents the necessary confrontational aspect of leadership where biblical correction is administered, where sin is confronted, and moral directions are changed. Just as a father disciplines his children, so a Christian leader needs to confront what is wrong in the church and guide people into what is right.

These are the three marks of leadership by which Paul identifies the leaders in Thessalonica, and which any and every church will always need. These are the people who prove themselves to be leaders. Christian leadership is not achieved by going to a college or taking a course, or by assuming a title or even by being elected to a position. True leadership is about doing a job and doing it conscientiously, honestly and Christianly. It means working hard, caring for people, and admonishing in love.

Response to true leadership

What response to that leadership is Paul looking for in the church? He uses another triplet here. He is looking for respect (v. 12) for 'those who work hard among you'. He wants the church to 'hold them in the highest regard' and 'to live in peace with each other' (v. 13).

The idea of 'respect' has an interesting and instructive framework of reference. Its literal translation is 'to know', which helps us to see why Paul uses it here. 'We ask you, brothers, to know those who work hard among you.' Clearly, this is not in the sense of knowing who they are, which would be transparently obvious, but in the sense of giving them proper recognition. A cross-reference from a leadership context again will help our understanding. In 1 Corinthians 16:15-18, Paul writes that Stephanas and his household have devoted themselves to serving the saints. He then urges the Corinthian church to submit to such as these, and to everyone who joins in the work and labours at it (v. 16). This is the same vocabulary of ministry which Paul uses in Thessalonians – labouring, joining in the work. He concludes, 'For they refreshed my spirit and yours also. Such men deserve knowing', or, as the NIV translates it, they deserve recognition (v. 18).

It is not a matter of status or privilege, but of respect for the worker because of his work. Those who work hard among the church must be 'recognised' as its leaders. They need to be acknowledged as such and treated accordingly. Of course, this accords with Paul's emphasis throughout the letter. It is not just the objective statement of truth, but the personal behaviour accompanying it which proves the reality. So the mere statement or designation of a person as a leader is meaningless unless it is accompanied by these qualities. But wherever these qualities are being exercised, where there is hard work, a willingness to confront, and a consistent love that is labouring and caring for the flock, then the command of verse 13 follows: 'Hold them in the highest regard in love because of their work.' They are to be recognised and considered 'exceedingly highly' (literally) because they are faithful leaders. As their service is motivated by love, so the church's response to them should be motivated by love.

Paul is asking not for grudging admission, but for glad recognition of God-given leaders, because of the functions they are fulfilling and the way they are carrying them out. That sort of attitude within the community will bring the peace which he asks for at the end of verse 13. Peace like that in the Christian community is a very powerful evangelistic persuader.

So, standing back from those two verses, what can we learn? Clearly in Thessalonica some struggles about leadership were developing, which is not so surprising in view of Paul's hasty withdrawal. There is a hint of the same problem a little later in verse 20, where we have the instruction, 'Do not treat prophecies with contempt.' This may mean that those who had a different view from Paul on various issues, such as the parousia and the most appropriate way of waiting for the Lord's return, were actually claiming prophetic authority for their heterodox teaching. That would lead to a devaluing of the prophetic ministry in a church where the New Testament canon was non-existent, and where the ministry of the apostles and prophets is foundational (Eph. 2:20, 3:5). Some may have been claiming prophetic authority for saying, for example, that the day of the Lord had already come. Immediately, that precipitates a crisis of leadership. How do you know who is right? Are you going to tolerate them standing up and teaching their views in the church's meetings? What about these idle people in verse 14, who may well be saying that they have been called to a ministry of waiting? Are they going to be allowed to do that, or is someone going to challenge it? Paul says that the idle have got to be warned, but that requires authority; it requires a recognised exercise and acceptance of leadership.

The interesting thing to me, however, is that Paul does not speak in structural but in functional terms. Leaders are to be recognised by their function. They are not imposed by the apostle. They have already emerged in the church, and if the qualities are being fulfilled, then the leadership is to be recognised. Even when Titus is told to ordain elders in every local church in Crete, he is not left without a list of qualities to look for. The leaders will already be emerging; he has simply to recognise them.

At present, we seem to be facing a crisis of leadership in many local congregations. One hears of a distressing number of churches, beset by squabbles and disagreements, in which Paul's teaching needs to be heard. Many of the problems concern leadership. Sometimes churches feel that leadership is being imposed from outside, rather than being proved and emerging from within. One of the problems we have in our structural set-up today is that some who are selected by denominational procedures for the full-time ministry have demonstrated none of the qualities which Paul looks for in the leadership of a gospel church. It is hardly surprising that when they come into a church as the leader they find that there is opposition to them. They do not work among the people; there is no care; there is no admonition from Scripture.

Those who are spiritually keen but are not recognised as leaders in that situation, then think that they must take matters into their own hands, and they will try to correct the situation or to fill the vacuum, often with disastrous results. An alternative leadership develops – 'We believe the Lord is saying that...' – party spirit flourishes and the church is soon divided and even at war with itself. All sorts of different issues can be used to light the fuse, but that is the all-too-familiar story.

Now Paul is saying that there must be leadership within the body of Christ and these functions have to be fulfilled. In a sense, ministry validates itself. A call to the ministry presupposes that these qualities are already characteristic of the person who is asking to be set aside for full time work. If such a person is not already working hard, caring for the flock, and seeking to admonish one another, then simply being called the Reverend Somebody isn't going to make an iota of difference. But where those ministries are being fulfilled within the church, those who fulfil them, whatever their title may or may not be, are to be respected and held in high regard, in love. There should be an evident unity and harmony expressive of the controlling peace of God in the midst of the congregation.

Correcting problems

Moving on to verse 14, we can see Paul starting to mend the holes in the net. He sees, in three distinct categories of people, problems developing in the church which will present a distinct threat to the wellbeing of the congregation. These are issues with which the leadership must deal. A number of the commentators think he is talking exclusively to the leaders in verse 14, when he writes, 'we urge you, brothers'. But he has used this form of address several times earlier in the letter, when clearly he is talking to the whole church. While it is true to say that leaders have a special responsibility to deal with these problems, Paul here involves the whole church in what is a mutual responsibility.

So, what are the problems that have to be addressed? Firstly, they are told, *'warn those who are idle'*. It is a negative word in Greek (*atactoi*) meaning disorderly, undisciplined or the loafers, as we might call them. It is used extensively in 2 Thessalonians 3, where he is dealing again with these people. 'Keep away from every brother who is idle and does not live according to the teaching you received from us' (2 Thess. 3:6). That is why admonition is important in a leader. He has to confront those who are not living in accordance with sound teaching. By contrast, Paul says, 'We were not idle when we were with you' (2 Thess. 3:7). That was why he and Silas and Timothy worked night and day rather than have the Thessalonians support them. And he says again, 'We hear that some among you are idle. They are not busy; they are busy-bodies' (2 Thess. 3:11). This term, idle, is used of a sentry who is not at his post, in direct contrast with 1 Thessalonians 5:8 where he writes about people being alert and self-controlled, properly armed for the battle. It is used of an army that is undisciplined, a rag-tag group of soldiers. If there are individuals or a group like that in the church they have to be warned, they have to be confronted and rebuked. A change in their behaviour must be demanded.

We know why, because all through the letter we have had an emphasis on work, especially 'that you work with your own hands ... so that your daily life may win the respect of outsiders' (4:11-12). It does seem, though, that the idle regarded themselves not as those who had to be rebuked, but as spiritually superior. They seem to have been only too willing to justify their idleness as 'waiting for the coming'. Not for them the activity of the missionary apostle. They were the special order of 'waiters', resting in the Lord, and preparing their own souls to be blameless at his appearing. If this was, as they claimed, the most spiritual way to live, it followed that other Christians should support them financially. Some perhaps even claimed prophetic authority to demand such support. You can imagine the church business meeting, can't you? 'The Lord has shown me that my calling is to be a humble 'waiter'. He has also shown me that you are called to provide me with what I need for this spiritual work, and I just happen to have here a pile of standing orders for you to complete.' Paul says this is creating a scandal, which the pagans see through without any difficulty. They write them off as parasites and spongers. But with that, they also write off the naïve and gullible Christians who give way to this pseudo-spiritual blackmail, so that the pagans are then happy to reject the gospel, because it produces such credulous weaklings.

The circumstances and claims may be different but we still have the idle with us today. What about those Christian television personalities with their multi-million dollar budgets and their heart-rending appeals to manipulate gullible people to support their lifestyles? The question that such need to be asked is clear: 'Are you actually working hard among God's people?' Most of them are totally inaccessible. 'Do you care for those you exploit?' Sometimes, it seems, very little. Then we have got to warn them.

But it happens at a local church level too. People receive 'pictures' or are 'given' Bible verses of what they imagine God is calling them to do, as though that were sufficient justification for others to support them financially. Every pastor knows what it is to be on the receiving end of that sort of thing. 'We don't know yet what specific ministry we are going to be involved in when we get to Acapulco, but we just feel we ought to be there for some time so that we can be led more clearly!' Warn those who are idle. There will be those who want to go out into the desert, or up to the mountain to wait for the Lord, but real Christianity serves the living and true God in his church and through his church. True Christians are distinguished by their labour and their hard work, and Satan will still make busybodies of those who are not busy in the Lord's business.

Secondly, *the timid are to be encouraged.* Here the word 'timid' is 'little-spirited' or 'faint-hearted'. Typically, people of this category are anxious, fearful, very easily despondent. They can quickly be shaken by opposition and persecution, and readily unsettled by all sorts of trials. Again we find many folk like that still in our congregations. It may be that this is a group particularly concerned about the questions that Paul dealt with in chapter 4, the relationship of the dead to the coming King. It would be typical of such folk to worry about whether the dead would enjoy the same advantages at the parousia as the survivors. Or they might be worried about the suddenness of the day of the Lord. Would they really be acceptable to him if he came suddenly? Would they be rescued from the coming wrath? Is their salvation secure? We are all familiar with that sort of timidity.

The use of the word 'encourage' hints that this was their special area of need, because it frequently means to console someone who is mourning. So the timid, who may be very worried about death and about the future and about all the uncertainties of the coming, need to be consoled. They may be the ones who were grieving without hope (4:13). What they need is fresh courage and confidence, which comes both by the clear teaching Paul has given them in the letter and also by a targeted ministry of encouragement and help directed specifically to them. That is something a leader will be doing as part of his hard work. In every church, there will be a few idle who have to be warned and admonished, but there will be many timid Christians whose faith needs to be taught and strengthened. The thrust of this is that inadequate and diffident Christians are not to be written off, but consoled and encouraged. Beware of any church or ministry that does not have time for the timid. If church leaders are interested only in going for the able, the elite, the storm troopers, as it were, then we have lost one of the great strands of New Testament Christianity.

Thirdly, *we must also be concerned for the weak*. 'Weak' is a term with the widest reference of meaning. It can mean sickly, financially bankrupt, or spiritually feeble. Probably, it was this group in Thessalonica who succumbed most easily to the prevailing climate of sexual immorality (4:3-8). It was tied up with the idolatry which permeated the culture. It would require real strength from an individual to break with this kind of sexual practice – and these were weak Christians. In pagan Greece, the temple was a dominating presence with its immorality and its idolatry. It would have been very tempting to take the line of least resistance, whether out of weakness, immaturity or inexperience. Afterwards, there was a perfectly respectable logical argument that could be use to justify their actions. The soul is the eternal reality which is imprisoned in the temporality of the body. So, because the body is going to decay anyway, it does not matter too much what one does with it. The pure spark within is what matters, and that will one day be liberated from the house of clay. Weak Christians could easily be taken in by that sort of casuistry. That is why in chapter 4 Paul taught the eternal significance of what is done in the body, 'the Lord will punish men for all such sins in the body' (4:6). Or again, 'He has given us his Holy Spirit in order to enable us to live holy lives in the body' (4:8). 'The dead in Christ will rise first' (4:16). The resurrection of the body confirms how important eternally the body really is. It is more than just a shell, much less a prison-house. It is an integral part of our total personhood as human beings. Paul's concern is that 'your whole spirit, soul and body be kept blameless at the coming of our Lord Jesus Christ' (5:23), and that is how the weak have to be helped. It is very easy to drift back into paganism. Christian consecration has to be ethical because there is no biblical spirituality that can be divorced from the body.

These, then, are the three areas which could threaten the church, and as a church together they must urge one another to live in the right way. The idle must be warned and made to work; the timid must be encouraged; the weak must be helped.

Personal relationships

Next, Paul directs the church to the distinctively Christian qualities of personal relationships. All this hard work, which is going on to admonish, strengthen and support, has certain gospel distinctives which mark it out not as a work of human effort, but as a work of God. Paul draws attention to three of them.

'Be patient with everyone' is the first (v. 14b). The idea of long-suffering introduced here has a great biblical pedigree, going right the way back to the character of God in Exodus 34:6. He is a God who is slow to anger. Patience is a fruit of his Spirit (Gal. 5:22). Love is patient (1 Corinthians 13:4); that is characteristic of *agape*. If Christians are going to live at peace with one another, they will need to be long-suffering, particularly as their leaders tackle the unending demands of pastoral work. We still need that sort of long-suffering, characterised by speaking gently but firmly, moving at the pace of the people we are helping, keeping on with the hard work, even when there seems to be no response. All this requires divine resources. No successful pastor-teacher is impatient. We have to take the long view. As Paul told Timothy, 'correct, rebuke and encourage – with great patience and careful instruction' (2 Tim. 4:2).

In these instructions, then, about being patient with everyone, whether they are the idle, timid, weak or whoever one is dealing with, it seems that the focus now begins to broaden even more. *'Make sure that nobody pays back wrong for wrong'* (v. 15). So, within the church, the relationships that mark the brothers out from the others include this sort of patience, this sort of loving care that goes on bothering, with the absence of revenge, that nobody pays back wrong for wrong. It was Sir Walter Scott who called revenge 'the daintiest morsel ever cooked in hell'. The opposite of patience is retaliation, but that is not an option for the Christian believer. It is never right to return in kind; it simply multiplies the evil. What is the remedy? Instead, always, regardless of the circumstances (there are no escape clauses in the small print here), try to be kind to each other and to everyone else. 'Try' is a strong word, meaning make it your aim, put your effort into it. We are to pursue what is good towards one another, and toward everyone. The 'good' is obviously what is to the advantage of others, which is why it is paraphrased 'be kind'. It is this consistent working for the good of others that Paul is working for. That is where patience leads and that is what stops revenge.

I find it interesting that Paul gives no incentive or motivation here at all. It is just a fundamental Christian concern for the wellbeing of everybody, whether they are within the community of believers or not. We must be patient with everyone (v. 14), kind to each other (that is in the church) and to everyone else (v. 15) outside as well. The community, then, is to be a living example of the transforming power of the gospel, but always with its eyes on the world outside, never merely self-regarding. Even though one of the epistle's themes is to delineate the difference between the Christians and the pagans, to assure the believers that their identity is totally different as a result of God's choice, there is never any hint here of the ghetto. The New Testament does not endorse the kind of separation which some-times afflicts our churches, where Christians want to cultivate holiness living apart from the world, in an hermetically sealed environment. That is never an option for Paul, who is looking outwards all the time. Their kindness, their love, the quality of their relationships are to be seen in and by the world, as well as in the church. Only then will the church continue to thrive and be the beacon light for the gospel, which God intended and made it to be.

Priorities of Christian lifestyle

The next triplet gives three priorities of Christian lifestyle: 'Be joyful always; pray continually; give thanks in all circumstances, for this is God's will for you in Christ Jesus' (v. 16-18). The Good News Bible translates, 'this is what God wants from your life in union with Christ Jesus' which makes the point well. What God wants from his people is the fulfilment of his will. The will conveys a double sense of both what he wants and of what he provides. That is the important thrust in the second part of verse 18. What he intends, he makes possible. We have already noted this pattern earlier. 'It is God's will that you should be sanctified' (4:3), that is why he has given his Holy Spirit (4:8). Here, it is not so much ethical behaviour that is in view, as the quality of our personal lives in relationship with God. All this is possible – rejoicing, praying and giving thanks – because Christians are 'in Christ Jesus'. It is only in union with him that the will of God is fulfilled in our lives and these aspirations become realities.

'Rejoice always' reminds the church of how they first received the gospel. 'In spite of severe suffering, you welcomed the message with joy given by the Holy Spirit' (1:6). If you are in Christ, with his Spirit within you, that joy is a characteristic of gospel believers, as indeed it was of Paul when he reflected on their firm stand in Christ and the gospel (3:9). The joy that comes at the beginning of the Christian life is a joy that is to stay through it all, because it is a product of our relationship with God through the gospel, and that does not change. We can rejoice 'always' (verse 16) because that relationship is always the same. And if there is a day when I don't have that sense of rejoicing, when I find it hard, it is because somehow I am not aware of the great blessings that are mine in the gospel and I am not, at that moment, actively trusting God. Instead, I am feeling sorry for myself and have my eyes turned inward rather than out towards God. As Wanamaker comments, 'To rejoice always is to see the hand of God in whatever is happening and to remain certain of God's future salvation.'[1]

Secondly, 'pray continually' (v. 17). Again, we have had this word before. Paul is both praying constantly for them in Thessalonica (1:3) and thanking God continually for them (2:13). Obviously, it cannot mean that he is doing it without interruption, but that our speaking to God in prayer should be our natural resource throughout the day as frequently as possible, so that it becomes the dominating factor of our lives. W. E. Sangster, the Methodist preacher who had such a great ministry at Westminster Central Hall during the Second World War, used to say that when he woke up every morning he would begin the day by saying, 'Good morning, Lord, and what are we going to do together today?' That may sound a little quaint to our ears, but it is that sort of praying constantly which is the mark of a godly spirit. It is that consciousness of God in every situation, which makes it the most natural reaction to turn to him and talk about it.

'Give thanks in all circumstances' (v. 18) because we see the hand of God at work in all the changing scenes of life and we know that he is bringing everything together for the fulfilment of his perfect will. Paul is not asking them to do what he does not do himself. You can trace it through the letter – he rejoices, he prays constantly, he gives thanks continually. 'Be a model of me as I am of the Lord,' he says. These are the marks of Christian lifestyle.

Christian discernment

Lastly, we come in verses 19-22 to the principles of Christian discernment. Turning from the perspective of individual responsibility, we are now back firmly in the corporate church context. The apostle sees two dangers which he counteracts with three positive commands. Obviously the dangers in verses 19-20 belong together. 'Putting out the Spirit's fire' is 'treating prophecies with contempt'. The figure of fire is often used in Scripture for the presence and activity of the Spirit and the translation 'Do not quench the Spirit's flame' is perhaps the best way of understanding it.

Verse 20 tells us how this was in danger of happening in Thessalonica. I have already outlined what I think is the historical background, and why despising inspired utterance (prophecy) would be a specific problem in the church. A very possible scenario is that the gift is being abused to justify either erroneous teaching about the coming, or the idle in their false behaviour patterns. The currency of prophecy would be devalued as a result. The gift was the ability to receive and communicate direct revelation from the Lord. Elsewhere, Paul says that 'everyone who prophesies speaks to men for their strengthening, encouragement and comfort' (1 Cor. 14:3). But if a prophet says that the day of the Lord has already come and the apostle denies it, who is to be believed? All prophecy would then risk being devalued.

We need to remember that New Testament prophecy, like its equivalent in the Old Testament, deals as much with present events as with predictive utterance about the future. If prophecy was rejected as a category within a church which was so dependent on it, then a major channel of revelation is going to be neglected.* Rather than throw the baby out with the bathwater, Paul gives three instructions as to how to deal with the situation. The first is 'test everything' (v. 21). We have met this verb (*dokimatzo*) earlier in the letter where we saw that it meant testing something, trying it out, proving it, and so approving of its use. It is commonly used of a money-changer testing the genuineness of a coin. That is the responsibility of the church. Every claim to inspired utterance has to be tested so that any counterfeit can be detected and exposed. The obvious way to do that would be by the Old Testament Scriptures and the apostolic teaching, or for us, by the whole Bible. So in application to us, we are right to test all that we hear or read by the word of God to determine

---

*Before the New Testament was written and the canon of Scripture complete, the church relied upon the verbal ministries of the apostles and prophets. Paul later explained, in Ephesians 2:20, 3:5 and 4:11, that these were foundation gifts, designed to communicate authoritatively the open secret (mystery) of the gospel, until God's written revelation was fully given.

whether it is in accordance with the complete and sufficient revelation of Holy Scripture.

Every preacher should say to the congregation, 'Don't believe this because I say it. Believe it because you see the Bible says it, and if you think the Bible does not say it, come and tell me. We are together under the authority of God's Word.' Every believer has that responsibility and privilege. Some will be more discerning than others. Young believers will need the instruction of older ones. The immature will need to be taught by the more mature. That is why what the prophets said had to be carefully weighed by their fellow prophets (1 Cor. 14:29), but it applies to us, equally, across the board, in all those things that we hear or read and take into our framework. We must test everything by the Word of God in order that we may hold on to the good and avoid every kind of evil, which is anything that runs contrary to the revealed will of God. Anything which is against the faith of the gospel, and the love that flows from that faith, all counterfeit teaching and living must be rejected and abandoned. It means that in our generation all pseudo-prophecies should be labelled as such and discarded. False teaching will always lead to wrong behaviour. It becomes the root for every kind of evil to develop within the church. So we have got to turn away from all that, and the only way we will do it effectively is by testing everything we hear against what God has already said and is still saying.

Closing benediction

We come now to the final prayer and the great assurance with which the letter ends. All through these instructions Paul is guarding the life of the church. He is giving them the parameters within which they can operate in faith, love and hope, and the means by which they can go forward. The final prayer encapsulates the purpose for all this. 'May God himself, the God of peace, sanctify you through and through. May your whole spirit, soul and body be kept blameless at the coming of our Lord Jesus Christ' (v. 23). Peace is the great gift of the gospel, the fruit of the Holy Spirit, and God himself is the source of this peace for his people. Paul's prayer is for thorough-going holiness in their lives, which, he says, is the work of the God of peace. He had prayed in 3:13 for God to 'strengthen their hearts so that they will be blameless and holy in the presence of God the Father when the Lord Jesus comes', and now the teaching in the chapters between has demonstrated the means by which that great purpose can be fulfilled. But in a characteristically Thessalonian reference, Paul stresses that it is the parousia which makes it such an urgent priority. It is, in the light of that day, the coming of our Lord Jesus Christ, that we need to be growing in holiness every day that we live. The God who provides peace is the God who is equally able to make his people holy. What Paul prays for is a sanctification that affects every part of the person – spirit, soul and body – all that is physical, all that is spiritual, so that at the parousia, in every department of life, the assessment will be 'blameless'.

It means that there is no legitimate ground for accusation. We have seen the idea in 2:10, where Paul describes the way he lived among them as 'righteous and blameless'. He has prayed for it in 3:13. It is to be found free from fault and that can only be by God's work in us. That is his will for us and it is the ultimate assurance of the certainty of our salvation.

Because this is supremely a letter of assurance and encouragement, Paul ends with a wonderful conviction in verse 24: 'The one who calls you is faithful and he will do it.' Isn't that a great note to end on? This is the only confidence we can have, given our human weakness, but it is the only confidence we need. The verb is a present participle – God is the one who 'is calling' you. It is not that God called us once in our salvation, but that he is continually calling us, all the time, calling us to salvation, calling us to sanctification, calling us to heaven. It mirrors the assertion at the beginning of the letter: 'God has chosen you' (1:4). How do I know he has chosen me? Because he is calling me. His Spirit is at work in me all the time, prompting me to an increase in faith and love and hope. That is the assurance that he will bring us home to glory. He will never withdraw his call, and we shall find him utterly faithful on that last great day. 'Those he justified, he also glorified' (Rom. 8:30). 'He who began a good work in you will carry it on to completion until the day of Christ Jesus' (Phil. 1:6). That is the ultimate assurance and it is the birthright of every child of God. It is the end point and purpose of the whole letter. What has been Paul's dominating concern now becomes the assurance of his closing prayer: God will bring his people into his presence, blameless at his coming. He has called you. He is calling you. 'He is faithful and he will do it.'

Our job is to keep on keeping on, as we cultivate love, faith and hope 'more and more'. Paul's great conviction is that his flagship church will be there on the last day, in the presence of the Lord Jesus, and by God's grace so shall we, if those same characteristics are demonstrated in our lives. For we also are God's people through faith in Jesus Christ, and we too are to live as demonstrations of a faith that works, a love that labours, and a hope that perseveres.

References

Chapter 1

1. Leon Morris, *The Epistle of Paul to the Thessalonians*, Tyndale New Testament Commentary Series, Inter-Varsity Press, London, 1956, p. 17.
2. Leon Morris, *1, 2 Thessalonians*, Word Biblical Themes, Word, Dallas, 1989, p. 3.
3. Charles A. Wanamaker, *Commentary on 1 & 2 Thessalonians,* New International Greek Testament Commentary, Paternoster, 1990, pp. 37-45.

Chapter 2

1. Ernest Best, *The First & Second Epistles to the Thessalonians*, Black's New Testament Commentaries, A & C Black, London, 1972, p. 67.
2. John Piper, *The Supremacy of God in Preaching*, Baker Books, Grand Rapids, 1990, p. 22.

Chapter 3

1. F F Bruce, *1–2 Thessalonians*, Word Biblical Commentary series, Word, Waco, 1982, p. 24.
2. Bruce, *op cit*, p. 26.
3. G G Findlay, *The Epistles to the Thessalonians*, Cambridge Greek Testament, Cambridge, C.U.P., 1925, cited in E Best, *op cit*, p. 101.

Chapter 5

1. Wanamaker, *op cit*, p. 146.
2. Norman H Snaith, *The Distinctive Ideas of the Old Testament*, Epworth Press, London, 1944, p. 21.
3. A B Davidson, *The Theology of the Old Testament* (1901), cited by Snaith, *op cit*, p. 12.

Chapter 6

1. Bruce, *op cit*, p. 96.
2. Morris, Tyndale New Testament Commentary, *op cit*, p. 87.

Chapter 7

1. Best, *op cit*, pp. 275-279.
2. Morris, Word Biblical Themes, *op cit*, p. 64.
3. Best, *op cit*, p. 208.

Chapter 8

1. Wanamaker, *op cit*, p. 200.

Also published by Christian Focus

Taking Jesus Seriously

The teaching of Jesus in Matthew

David Jackman

David Jackman explains the background and significance of the teachings of Jesus as recorded by his apostle, Matthew. In the Gospel of Matthew, there are five major teaching sections: the Sermon on the Mount (chapters 5-7); the commissioning of the Twelve (chapter 10); the parables of the Kingdom (chapter 13); the life of the kingdom community (chapter 18); an eschatalogical discourse (chapters 24-25). In his Gospel, Matthew interacts with Old Testament teachings and predictions as he presents Jesus as God's King. The author is aware of recent scholarly research into the possibility that Matthew originally wrote in Hebrew, and that it is helpful to translate the Greek text into Hebrew in order to get a fuller understanding of Jesus' teachings.

Don Carson comments on this book: 'Believers who work through this fine summary of what Jesus taught, will find their minds informed, their wills strengthened, their vision clarified and their hearts engaged.'

And Steve Gaukroger says: 'This book contains thorough, helpful and important material about the most significant character in history – Jesus of Nazareth.'

ISBN 1 85792 066 X   160 PAGES

Understanding the Church

David Jackman

Important aspects of the life of the church are explained, such as evangelism, worship, teaching, and discipline. The discussion of each topic is firmly rooted in an appropriate passage from the New Testament

ISBN 185792 257 3   large format   208 pages

'I'm glad to recommend a careful study of this book, not just because David Jackman is a valued friend of mine, but because on this important matter of *Understanding The Church* he deserves to be heard. He has the two qualifications that are most necessary; a first-hand knowledge of pastoring a growing church for a number of years, and a first-rate capacity for handling scripture. Here are a dozen or more key Bible passages unlocked and applied, of which something like half come from that electrifying account of Word and Church growth in the Acts of the Apostles. Lively instruction of this kind will help churches to speed on rejoicing. Sound instruction like this will help churches to keep on the rails!'

Dick Lucas